THE CHALK TALK MANUAL

A Complete Presentation of the Theory and Practice of
this Fascinating Form of Entertainment

by
HARLAN TARBELL
Professional Magician and Entertainer

Publishers
T. S. DENISON & COMPANY, INC.
Minneapolis

CONTENTS

ILLUSTRATIONS

ILLUSTRATIONS—*Continued*

ILLUSTRATIONS—*Continued*

SECTION TWO—Fun with Chalk Talk

ILLUSTRATIONS

ILLUSTRATIONS—*Continued*

SECTION THREE—Chalk Talk Stunts

ILLUSTRATIONS

ILLUSTRATIONS—*Continued*

ILLUSTRATIONS *(Concluded)*

INTRODUCTION

RAWN lines are simple things in themselves, yet what a power of expression in a few of them appropriately combined! A few strokes of a cartoonist's pencil produces a stronger editorial than could be put into a column of type. The talent is not artistic, in the strict sense of that term. It seems to belong to the domain of psychology—a peculiarly penetrating psychology. From an art standpoint, frequently it is little better than the glyphs, ideographs and other crude drawings that have come down to us from savage or prehistoric man; yet like those elemental expressions from which a history is being traced, it tells amazingly much in amazingly small space.

A man may train his face into what he conceives to be a perfect mask. He may hide his character and emotions; until a keen cartoonist gets to work upon him. By emphasizing a feature or even exaggerating a bald spot, the man's inner nature seems to be revealed. The astonishing thing is the general accuracy of the revelation. Through some inexplicable mystery the cartoon conveys more to us concerning the individual than his private secretary, minister or physician could tell. The uncanny insight and keen expression of even the average cartoonist or chalk talker seems to suggest that they are under the protection and tutelage of a special set of fairies or hobgoblins.

Amiable as the talent generally is, it has been known to wreck political parties, uncrown kings and defeat presidents. A piece of chalk operated on white paper by a gentle individual so timid as to be afraid to go home in the dark, has more potentialities for havoc than a thousand cannons. Conversely, it has equal potentialities for construction, instruction, illustration and entertainment—especially for entertainment. The ears of an auditor may be dulled by words, but his eyes are never dulled by a striking picture. The more novel it is, the more it stirs his mind. If it has humor, associated with an idea, the effect is even greater. If it is merely funny without conveying any particular idea, it still has entertainment value.

Survivals from the stone age and even earlier periods indicate that picture making was one of the earliest modes of human expression. It must have been almost coeval with the formation of speech. The ability to draw, latent though it be, exists in every individual. It is one of the early manifestations of the child. His first markings are no less crude than his first attempts to talk. Because it is more essential to cultivate speech than draftsmanship, we have more talkers than draftsmen. If it were necessary to make out thoughts and our wants known by drawing pictures of them, every person would be an artist. And every person is a potential artist.

These observations are in keeping with the character of this book. It is offered, not as a manual of art, but as a practical guide to chalk talking, cartooning and plain illustrating. We feel that almost anyone who follows its clear rules and practices its easy, correct models will acquire the ability to deliver an entertaining chalk talk or to improve by illustrations the effect of a serious discourse.

THE PUBLISHERS.

Section I
HOW TO CHALK TALK

THE PRINCIPLES OF CHALK TALKING

Chalk talking, in its primary sense, consists of the quick execution of crayon drawings or sketches which illustrate graphically and in a novel manner the points which the speaker is conveying. It is used either for serious expression or as a form of entertainment.

The field of the chalk talk is unlimited. It can be employed to advantage wherever there is need for public expression. The chalk talk can be made of far-reaching service in business and professional life —for salesmanship, educational and religious work as well as for entertaining. It is an accomplishment of tremendous value not only for the entertainer but likewise for the teacher, the clergyman, the salesman, the lecturer, the public speaker on any subject—in short, for anyone who has a message to convey.

The tremendous power of the picture as an adjunct to the spoken or written word is now so widely recognized that it need not be argued here. The newspaper publisher, the magazine editor, the advertising agency, all make ever-increasing use of illustrating as a means of conveying the ideas they express. The reason for the power of the picture is very simple. Vision is one of the primary mental processes. Describe a certain dog to a group of a dozen people and you will create a dozen different mental images, no two of them identical. Show them a picture of the dog, however, and they will all know precisely the kind of a dog you are talking about.

The average person who speaks in public gives little thought to the possibilities of strengthening his talk with chalk, because he has an idea that chalk talking requires an artistic genius which he does not possess.

To dispel that illusion, let it be stated emphatically at once that chalk talking is not necessarily a gift. It is an accomplishment, and a fair ability at chalk talking may be acquired by a person who is not naturally gifted as an artist, just as surely as a fair ability at piano playing may be acquired by a person who is not naturally musical.

In the present volume, chalk talking is discussed primarily from the angle of its value as a medium of entertaining, for both professionals and amateurs, be they on the vaudeville stage or the lyceum or chautauqua platform, in parlor-entertaining or club work or in the ever-widening home-talent field.

One of the secrets of the chalk talk's strong appeal is the fact that the audience sees the picture built up line by line. It arouses curiosity as to the finished result. It is a story told to the eye as well as to the ear. Like the novel and like the stage play, it grips the beholder because it arouses tense interest, creates and maintains suspense and often has a sudden and unexpected outcome. Like the novel and the play again, it may range from comedy to tragedy. It may evoke either smiles or tears. Because of these very human qualities the chalk talk may be employed to convert what might otherwise be a dull or uninteresting talk or lecture into a presentation of powerful appeal.

Since the chalk talk embraces two media of expression, it follows that generally one of these media dominates the other. That is, the chalk is used to intensify the talk, or else the chalk creates the main appeal and the talk is subsidiary to it. In the field of entertaining, the audience generally is interested primarily in the chalk—what it sees—and the talking is merely an accessory. So true is this that the gifted artist may dispense with his talk, or "patter," entirely, and employ a musical accompaniment instead so that it is all chalk and no talk. In other words, the chalk does the talking. The inexpert chalk talker, however, will generally find that the use of appropriate comment, or "patter," in connection with his presentations will be of material aid in winning his audience. The problem of patter, therefore, as well as the creation of the drawings themselves, is given due consideration in the following pages.

As already suggested, the average person holds back from essaying the chalk talk field because he does not know that its principles are within his grasp. Unfortunately, there has been little information written on the subject. And if a clever chalk talker is regarded as the possessor of some rare gift, not accessible to the average mortal, it may be that he makes little effort to correct the impression.

Throughout this book pictures and effects have been developed to show the construction of pictures and the creation of effects with a saving of effort and time. That is the value of the evolution picture, where there is a quick change from one picture to another by adding a few lines; also the upside-down picture, where a picture is transformed into another by merely reversing its position. This style of drawing is not only a time-saver, but adds considerable interest because it is unexpected and out of the ordinary. It carries a power of entertainment that must

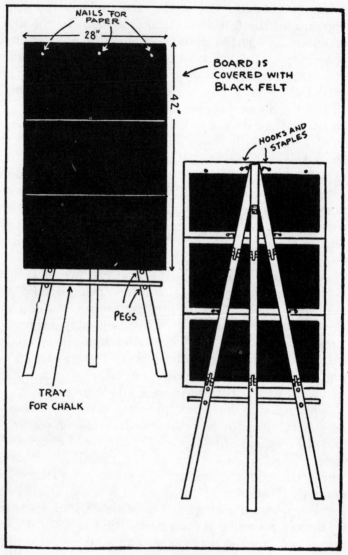

PLATE 1
Drawing Board and Easel

not be overlooked. No matter how serious a subject may be, it must be presented in an interesting and entertaining style to gain for it the greatest effect.

After studying the various methods and effects employed throughout this book, the lecturer or the entertainer will find ways of adapting them to meet his individual needs.

CHALK TALK MATERIALS.

The author's chalk talk equipment consists of the following:

Folding easel.

Folding drawing board (28x42 inches).

Tray for chalk.

Lecturer's crayons.

Small boxes of powdered crayon for landscape and blended background effects.

Several wads of cotton for blending colors.

White paper (newspaper stock, size 28x42 inches).

Various colored papers (which act as a medium tone for high-light and deep shadow effects).

Plates 1, 2 and 3 show parts of the equipment.

The folding easel, board and tray described are practical and serviceable. The outfit is handy for carrying, since it packs small. A large canvas cover or suitcase should be used to carry the folded outfit.

A stick of lecturer's crayon, or chalk, is shown in Plate 3. This can be trimmed or cut down to fit various requirements. Crayon comes in many colors and shades. The large art stores are usually stocked with these chalks. Black and white are the cheapest

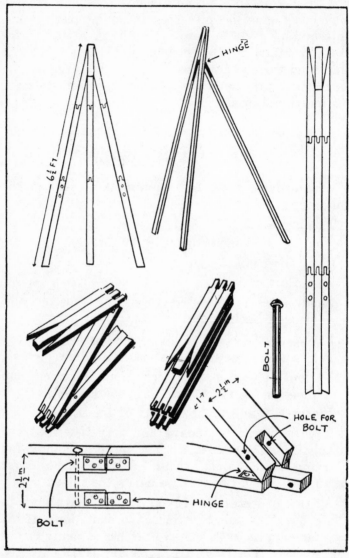

PLATE 2
Details of Easel

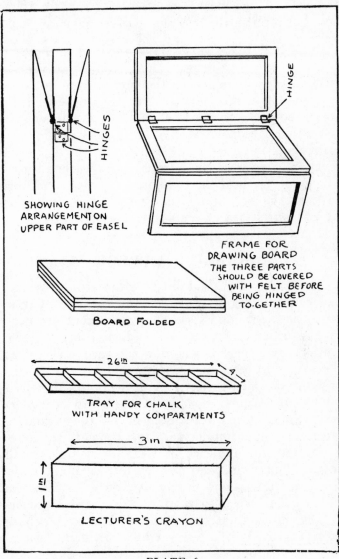

SHOWING HINGE
ARRANGEMENT ON
UPPER PART OF EASEL

FRAME FOR
DRAWING BOARD
THE THREE PARTS
SHOULD BE COVERED
WITH FELT BEFORE
BEING HINGED
TO·GETHER

BOARD FOLDED

TRAY FOR CHALK
WITH HANDY COMPARTMENTS

LECTURER'S CRAYON

PLATE 3
Further Details of Equipment

and the reds the most expensive. Some chalk artists buy a complete assortment. Others use only a few colors.

Individual taste varies in regard to a choice of paper on which to draw. Choice ranges all the way from newsprint paper to the high grade book papers and chalk talk papers. Practical experience has shown, however, that a fair grade of newspaper stock is the most economical, the easiest to obtain (any print shop or paper house carries it), the lightest to carry, and answers the purpose for all-around work. The paper is held on the board by means of three nails at the top of board, or by large clips which may be purchased at a stationery store.

ARRANGING A PROGRAM.

Arranging a chalk talk program is a great deal like constructing a play for the theatre. Certain dramatic points and style of arrangement are necessary in order to interest the audience, hold their attention and accent where necessary. There are climaxes and secondary climaxes.

There must be variety. A program of all comedy would not be good, nor would one of all heavy dramatic work. Contrast is needed. Through contrast comedy becomes funnier and tragedy more thrilling.

The average audience tires easily. People usually crave stimulation, and the performer must understand enough about psychology to know how fast to work and when to change. Vaudeville audiences in large cities usually want things done very rapidly. They are used to a hurried life. In more leisurely communities, one should work more leisurely and give opportunity for meditation. The chautauqua chalk talker works with less speed than does the vaudeville man. One must always study the psychology of the audience, and consider the best form of gaining and holding interest for the particular subject introduced.

In opening a program it is well to use a novelty picture, one that can be drawn quickly, that carries a laugh, and offers a quick surprise that makes people interested at the very start. There must be something to break the ice, putting the performer and the audience on friendly terms. Should the lecture be scientific and of such nature as to hold the spectators on a tension, this tension should be relieved occasionally with a snappy novelty picture that puts people in good humor.

Colored landscapes and pictures that take several minutes' time should be followed by pictures that take but a moment. Avoid long drawn out programs.

To close a program, again study the construction of a play or playlet. An audience wants to leave well satisfied and happy. No matter how many tears you have brought forth during the program, the end should show that all is well and "they lived happily ever after." A good story can end in tragedy, but it takes highly skilled construction in order to leave a good impression. The safest way, as a rule, is to close with a note of good cheer.

A short program that is planned for an encore should close with a bang. The best work possible should be thrown into the closing picture. Make the audience wonder at the skill of the performer or the impressiveness of the subject. Vaudeville, especially, demands work of this nature, for a good round of applause is what many managers are guided by in judging an act.

For a longer or full-evening program the climax or punch may occur before the end, and the closing subject may be of such a nature to "smooth things over." Sometimes a picture drawn to illustrate a poem, and accompanied by music, is effective. At other times the artist may use some little novelty indicating the end by a hearty Good-Night.

The opening and closing of a program are highly important, and may mar or make a finished performance.

The length of a program depends on conditions. A program may run from ten minutes to an hour and a half. It is as bad to overdo as to underdo. The novice usually tends to run over his time, and to crowd too many things into a program. It is better to simplify and to close exactly at the moment set. The advice oftentimes given to a beginner is to figure on the amount of a program he would like to give, then to cut it in half.

The amount of experience that a chalk talker has had is also a factor. Practice makes perfect, and a program that would answer the purpose in the beginning might become too short later on. Or even a program normally of the proper length might take too long to give on the opening night. The experienced chalk talker finds that a colored landscape, which he rushed through in twenty minutes on his first attempt, becomes an easily drawn three-minute picture after he has presented it several times. It is wise to rehearse several times before presenting a program until one gets trained in extemporaneous work. Rehearsing and trying things out enables one to see the flaws that only experience can reveal. An arrangement which theoretically ought to be excellent may prove impractical when put to the test of actual use.

In going before an audience the things you counted on most to gain your point may fall the flattest. Sometimes a little thing, apparently insignificant, gets the most attention. Your comedy may prove sad, and your sad points may be the laugh of the evening. Experience eventually gives one "sure-fire material" that can be fallen back on in emergencies, but this sure-fire presentation only comes through experience. This book is made up of material that has proven "sure-fire" for the author in actual use.

IMPORTANT POINTS.

Chalk talking should be simple. Use the fewest lines possible to bring out an idea at its best.

If you want to be sure of a picture that seems difficult, outline it in advance with a lead pencil. The lines, if made lightly, will not be noticeable even a few feet away, but they will be easily seen by the chalk artist. It is easy to chalk over the pencil outlines. This preliminary drawing before your program starts is oftentimes a regular life saver. It is a splendid aid for the beginner to give him assurance, and for the man who does not have the time to practice up on pictures and who does not feel capable of presenting them extemporaneously. It is in reality a method similar to that of the pen-and-ink artist who draws first in pencil and inks over it, or the one who puts on oil paint over his charcoal sketch. The audience is, of course, not informed of the preliminary pencil lines.

Chalk is a rather dirty thing to handle, and it is easy to soil the hands and clothes. Some chalk

PLATE 4
Facial Expressions Simplified

artists wear gloves, but gloves, unless of fine texture, tend to destroy a person's sense of touch. A good way is to cover the end of each stick of chalk with tin foil and touch only the part so protected. When working with the bare chalk, it is wise to prepare by putting talcum powder on the hands in advance. This aids in the removal of chalk from hands with soap and water afterward. Another method is to cold cream the hands well before starting, and then to use cold cream in removing chalk from hands, as an actor does in applying and removing his make-up. The final cleanup is made with soap and water.

It is advisable to put a sheet of paper on the floor if working in a home or in any place where there are carpets or rugs. The chalk dust is hard to clean from carpets.

Practice your pictures on a small scale with a pencil before attempting to make them full sized. Get the pictures firmly in mind before making them with chalk. One can start work on a large sheet with chalk at once, if desired, but the smaller renditions for practice will save useless expense.

In public presentation, keep the pictures fairly large and make the lines heavy enough. They should be plainly and easily seen by persons in the rear of the hall. It is not necessary to work delicately, for distance lends enchantment to chalk talk pictures just as it does to stage scenery.

Stand at the side of the board rather than in front, in order to allow the audience to see as much as possible of each line that is made. Clear vision of your movements step by step prevents attention from lagging.

After finishing the various stages of the picture, stand aside and give the audience plenty of time to

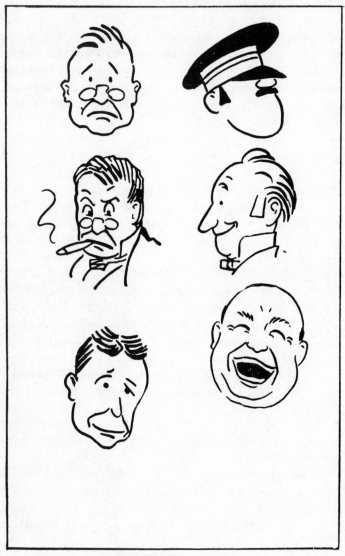

PLATE 5
Typical Facial Expressions

see what has been done. After the picture is finished, stand aside and allow a longer pause to give the audience a full view. In order that a picture may be fully comprehended, a chalk artist sometimes uses two easels, and works on them alternately, letting a finished picture remain on one while he works on the other. Or he may hang the finished picture upon a rack or special stand.

Keep your audience guessing. Endeavor to fill in the explanatory part of the picture last. Curiosity heightens interest.

When removing pictures from easel after they are finished, it is best to lay them carefully aside, as there are usually many calls for the pictures after the lecture. This is especially true in full evening entertainments or on club and chautauqua programs, where the artist may come in contact with his audience after the entertainment or lecture. A chalk drawing, however, has little or no permanent value, because it requires a special shellacking process in order to keep it from smudging. The drawings are so mussy to care for, and so easy to make, that the experienced chalk talker casts them aside if they are not demanded as souvenirs.

HINTS ON COLOR.

In the selection of colored chalk the artist should study the effect of each color under varying conditions of light and distance. A color that may show up well in daytime may create a sad effect under artificial light at night. Under artificial light the yellows tend to disappear and show as white. In fact, on a dark background yellow is often used for

PLATE 6
More Facial Expressions

white because of its better covering qualities and its brightening effect.

Orange is usually substituted for yellow at an evening performance when white paper is used, and when the performer is working with bold colors and not making a landscape.

Watch the effect of distance on color. Go to the rear of a theatre or hall and see what happens to your colored drawing on the stage. An apparently powerful combination may become quite subdued.

The chalk artist usually strives for strong contrasts and bright, live colors, to give his pictures a stimulating influence. At times the artist will work in subdued tones and then create a powerful contrast for the finish with high-lights and deep shadows. That the average audience likes strong contrast of well-chosen and combined color is shown by their appreciation of ripples on the water, lights shining from windows and other high-lighted scenes.

A good sized wad of cotton will help blend colors when subdued outlines are desired.

FACIAL EXPRESSIONS.

Chalk drawing aims to get an effect with as few lines as possible. This is particularly true of facial expressions. In drawing faces, study very carefully the effects that can be obtained by just a few lines properly arranged. Plate 4 gives eight effects expressing common emotions. To create laughter, the lines of the mouth turn upward at the corners. The heartier the laugh is, the more the mouth opens and the eyes close. In winking an eye the lines on one side of the face tend to pull together. Sadness and pessimism pull the corners of the mouth downward

PLATE 7
Still More Faces

and cause the eyebrows to accent themselves just above the nose. Surprise or fear tends to open the eyes and pucker up the mouth. Plate 4 is for training and practice rather than for public presentation. Plates 5, 6 and 7 show typical facial expressions and the lines used to make them.

In work of this kind, study the technique of well known cartoonists, as well as that of the caricaturist who make the comic sections of the Sunday newspapers.

EVOLUTION PICTURES.

This style of novelty drawing has an excellent effect on an audience because it keeps people guessing. It takes a picture which apparently is completed and transforms it into something else. The various steps from one picture to another create a mystery or suspense which heightens interest up to the very end. In the following pages there are given various examples of this type of work from a variety of angles and in different methods of treatment. In almost any sort of a program where a punch or a comedy effect is needed, an evolution picture will come to the rescue. Because of the few lines employed, such a picture can be brought to a rapid completion and the point be driven home quickly.

PATTER FOR EVOLUTION PICTURES.

The patter or talk that has been designed to accompany some of the drawings has been arranged from the entertainer's standpoint. It is to be accented, hastened or retarded according to develop-

PLATE 8
The Monkey and the Cat

ment of the drawing. Patter and drawing must fit. The artist can make a drawing, then talk, draw some more, then talk again. It is easier for the beginner to do this, for it takes a bit of experience to talk and draw smoothly together. In the following patter for the evolution pictures it is suggested to start talking after figure one has been drawn, then to deliver the closing punch line or lines as the performer steps away from the finished picture of figure four.

The Monkey and the Cat (Plate 8)

Upon a fence a monkey stood,
Just as a monkey sometimes would;
To sing and dance, and chin and chat
To a friend of his, a nearby cat.

The Windmill and Hans (Plate 9)

The windmill's wheel goes round and round,
So a farmer's wheat to flour is ground.
As it turns around it gives much joy
To little Hans, the miller's boy.

The Rabbit and the Magician (Plate 10)

(*Draw hat.*) Whenever I see a stovepipe hat, or a plug hat, or a small boy's delight in the winter time, as such a hat is sometimes called, it reminds me of my boyhood days when a magician came to town (*draw rabbit*) and found a white rabbit tucked away in a man's hat (*remove paper, turn it around and fasten to board again*) and turned the hat over and dumped Mr. Rabbit out. I never did understand how empty space could be turned into a rabbit until I ran across some magic chalk. Now I can go the old magician one better (*finish picture*) by changing the rabbit into the old magician himself.

PLATE 9
The Windmill and Hans

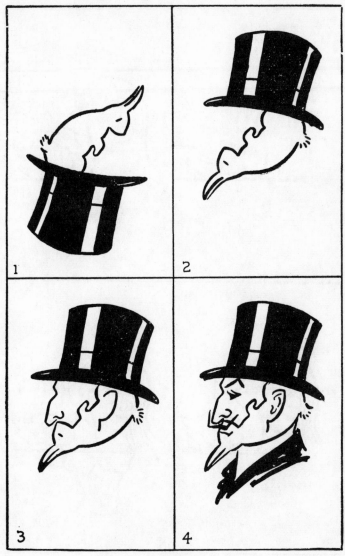

PLATE 10
The Rabbit and the Magician

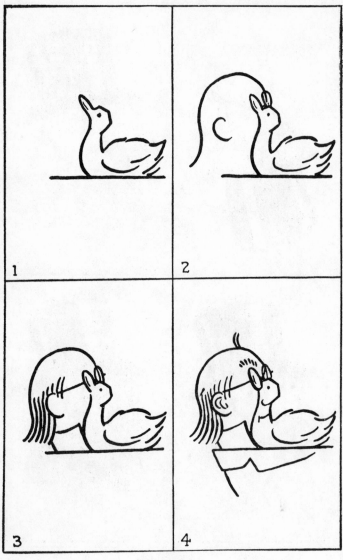

PLATE 11
The Duck and the Farmer

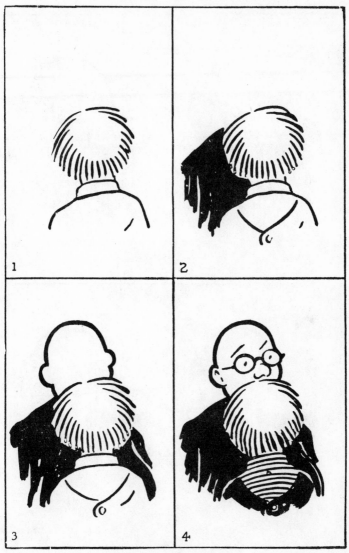

PLATE 12
Grandpa's Experience

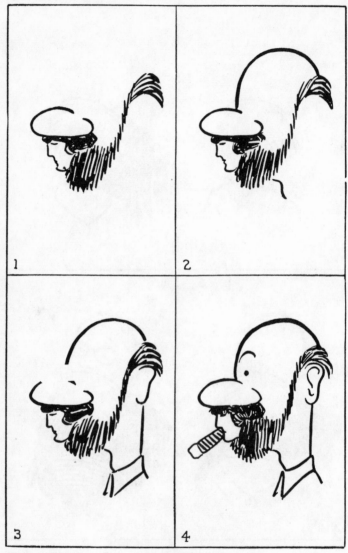

PLATE 13
A Lady and Her Husband

The Duck and the Farmer (Plate 11)

A duck swam round, down in a pond,
  A lookin' for his supper—
A nice big dish of oats or corn
  Fixed up by Farmer Tupper.

Grandpa's Experience (Plate 12)

When grandpa was a little boy
  A lot of hair grew on his head;
But now it's walked down on his chin—
  At least, that's what my grandpa said.

A Lady and Her Husband (Plate 13)

Because of the rapid change of styles, a man has
to have a daily report to be able to present a lady
in her proper costume. Furs, however, are always
safe, especially on a hot summer day, because styles
are now worn six months ahead of time. Yes, woman
is quite a puzzle. She has puzzled me for the last
eighty years. Now, for instance, can anyone here
tell me why such a pretty woman will pick out a
dumbbell like this for a husband?

Fido and the Tramp (Plate 14)

Under the spreading chestnut tree
  The family watch dog lies,
And now and then he wags his tail
  To shoo away the flies.
He sleeps and dreams the whole day through
  Upon the front door step;
But if a tramp comes into view
  Old Fido's full of pep.

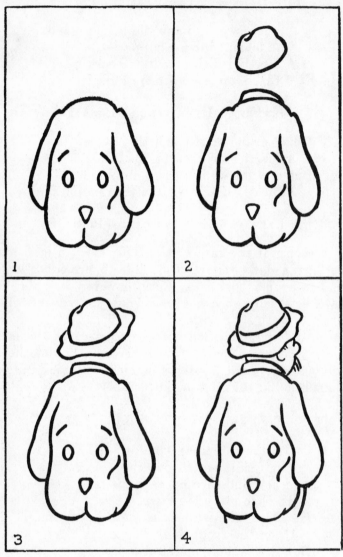

PLATE 14
Fido and the Tramp

PLATE 15
The Hired Man and the Farmer

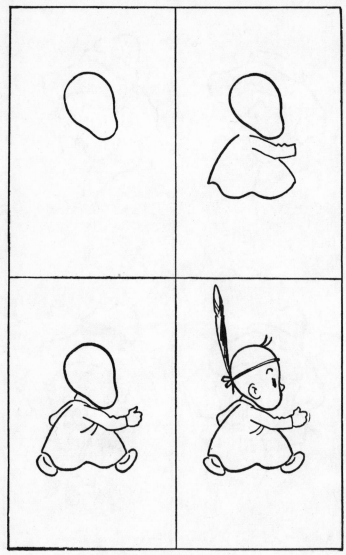

PLATE 16
The Pear and the Papoose

THE HIRED MAN AND THE FARMER (Plate 15)

This is a hired man. He is so lazy the farmer who hires him has to sharpen all the stumps on the place to keep him from sitting down most of the day. One day the hired man took it into his head to get his picture taken. This is it. When the farmer's wife saw the picture she said to her husband, "John, why don't you have your picture taken, too? I'd like to hang it up in the parlor." "You don't have to go to so much bother," said the hired man. "You can use one of mine." Then the farmer got mad and exclaimed, "Sufferin' punkins, who'd want your face in the parlor?" "No, no," said the hired man. "Not my face—yours." So saying, he took forth his pencil and— Now look what hangs around in the parlor; a picture of the farmer himself.

THE PEAR AND THE PAPOOSE (Plate 16)

A pear that grew upon a tree,
Away up high as high could be,
Dropped suddenly down on the ground to play
With a little papoose who ran away.

THE MOUSE AND THE LADY (Plate 17)

Once on a time a sociable mouse
Called at a maiden lady's house.
In fact, 'twas just a neighborly call;
A chair—a scream—and that was all.

THE PIG AND THE WOLF (Plate 18)

You have heard about "the little pig who went
to market
And the little pig who stayed at home
About the little pig who had roast beef
And the little pig who had none."

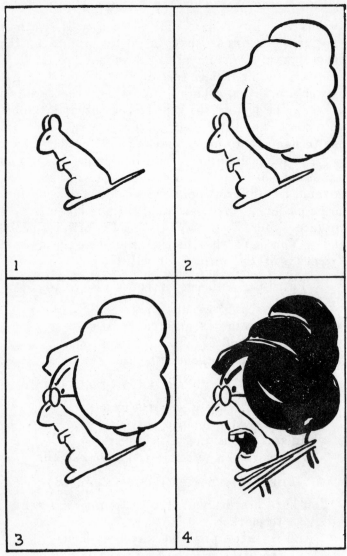

PLATE 17
The Mouse and the Lady

PLATE 18
The Pig and the Wolf

PLATE 19
The Palm Tree and the Hottentot

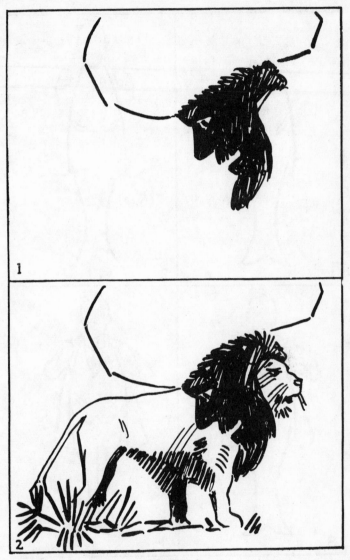

PLATE 20
The Hunter and the Lion

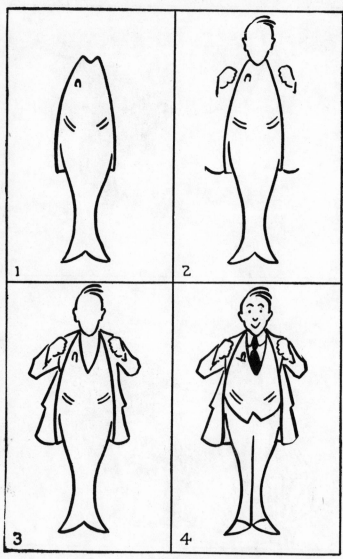

PLATE 21
The Fish and the Man

Well, this is the little pig who went "Wee-wee-wee!"

> For late at night
> When the wind would howl
> Little pig stayed at home
> Lest a wolf might prowl.

THE PALM TREE AND THE HOTTENTOT (Plate 19)

> Away down south in the South Sea isles
> There lived a big palm tree.
> Though it grew far away in a foreign land
> 'Twas a mighty fine tree for a palm leaf fan—
> Haw-haw! Ha-ha! Hee-hee!

> Under the tree when the sun got hot
> You could see, if you looked, a big black spot;
> It was twice as big as a big black blot;
> You can see, can you not, the Hottentot?

THE HUNTER AND THE LION (Plate 20)

There was an old hunter in Africa whose face was as black as coal and his turban as blue as the sky. He used to take with him a boy who seemed to have an uncanny sense of finding and routing out the numerous animals. One day the boy slipped quietly away from the side of the hunter. The latter heard a noise in the underbrush nearby and said, "Boy, come here." No answer. Again he called. Still no answer. "Ah, trying to fool me into thinking you are not there. But I hear a noise. Come out, you are just a lyin'." Then a head burst into view He was right, all right. It was just a lion.

THE FISH AND THE MAN (Plate 21)

> Papa caught a little fish,
> Mama put it in a pan,

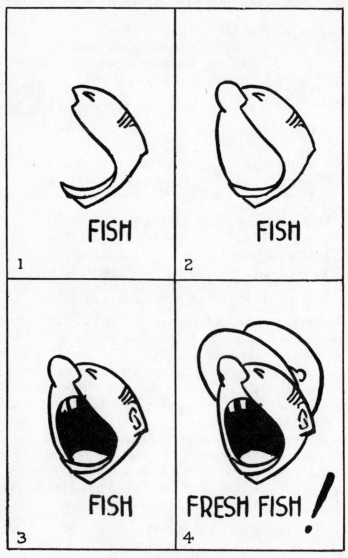

PLATE 22
The Fish and the Peddler

Sister put it on a plate—
And now the fish is in a man.

THE FISH AND THE PEDDLER (Plate 22)

This is the kind of a picture where the performer can substitute the written language for the spoken. After the fish is drawn (figure 1), letter the word "Fish" under it. When the peddler is finished (figure 4), step aside and leave the audience with the impression that you have finished the picture. Then turn suddenly to the board and write in the word FRESH in front of FISH, with an exclamation mark as the finale.

However, if patter is desired the following will fit in. (After drawing figure 1) "This is a fish—a F-I-S-H fish." (Draw figure 2.) "This is still a fish —it being known as the Woofus Fish—getting its name from the Greek word Woof-woof, meaning 'Get the hook.'" (Draw figure 3.) "It is still fish—only this time a cross between a kippered herring and a shrimp." (Draw figure 4.) "Fresh Fish!"

UPSIDE-DOWN PICTURES.

Upside-down pictures have a charm all their own because of the sudden and unexpected effects created. They embrace not only the interesting work of making a picture, but a surprise finish also. The audience thinks it sees the finished picture when the performer stops, but when he turns it upside down and another and entirely different effect magically appears, a new climax is reached. Plates 23 to 26 are given as examples of upside-down pictures. Each is simple in construction but very effective in the final change.

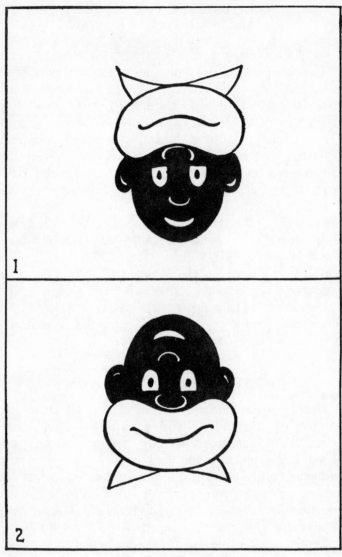

PLATE 23
Mandy and Rastus

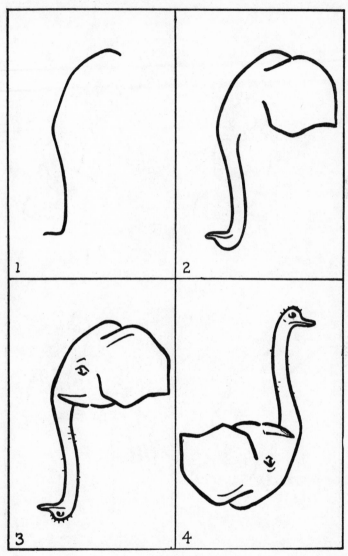

PLATE 24
The Elephant and the Ostrich

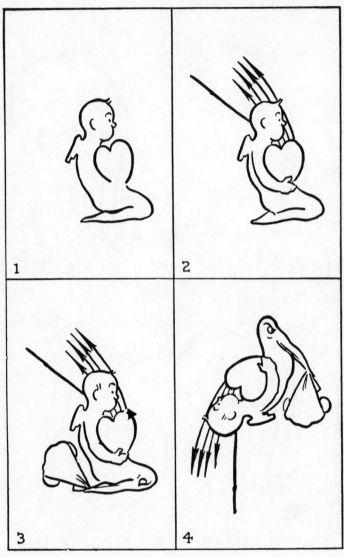

PLATE 25
Cupid and the Stork

Mandy changes to Rastus simply by turning the paper upside down (Plate 23); likewise the elephant to the ostrich (Plate 24); Cupid to the stork carrying the baby (Plate 25), and the river scene to the farm (Plate 26). The latter should be drawn in colors. The cabin of the houseboat should be white with the boat itself bright red and the roof black. The foliage of the trees may be drawn in dark green, with the trunks of the trees black or dark brown. Or both foliage and trunks may be drawn in the same color.

The change of Cupid to the stork (Plate 25) re-quires but a part turn of the paper to the left.

In making upside-down pictures, step aside from board long enough to give your audience a clear view of the first picture, then lift the paper from the board and hold it up, drawing attention to what the picture represents. Then turn the paper upside down and hold it long enough for the people to grasp fully what has happened. After this it is wise to hang the picture on a side easel or frame and leave it exposed to view while the next chalk drawing is being made.

PATTER FOR UPSIDE-DOWN PICTURES.

MANDY AND RASTUS (Plate 23)

A mighty fine girl is Mandy Brown
    The best wash lady for miles around
She never has a chance to shirk
    For Rastus finds her lots of work.
Mandy says, "Me and Rastus is just opposites."

THE ELEPHANT AND THE OSTRICH (Plate 24)

I was at a circus not long ago and there I met an

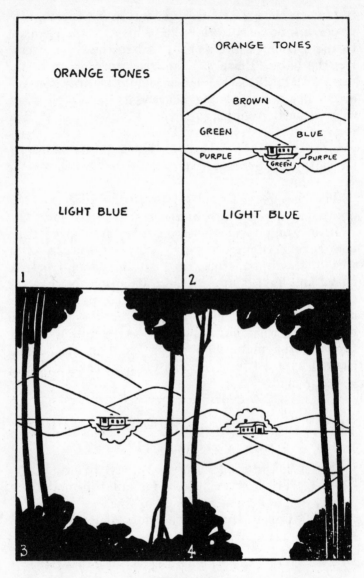

PLATE 26
The River and the Farm

old friend, Eddie Jumbo Elephant. He wiggle-waggled the snoot of his trunk around and took in enough peanuts to make a monkey jealous. Suddenly Eddie stopped and looked straight ahead for a few moments. "What's the matter, Eddie?" I asked.

Then the elephant said, "Upon my word—
But that ostrich is a funny bird."

Cupid and the Stork (Plate 25)

Well, I declare! Here's old friend Cupid;
Some folks says he is very stupid.
But with a heart and arrows few
It's few things that this boy can't do.

And now here's Cupid's second cousin—
He may bring one, or he may bring a dozen.

The River and the Farm (Plate 26)

When possible draw a picture of this kind to musical accompaniment. It fits nicely also with poetry.

THE EVOLUTION OF GIRLS' NAMES.

The chalk talker asks anyone in the audience to call out a girl's name. This he writes on the paper. Then with a few lines he changes the written name into a picture of a girl.

The name really helps to form, or does form, the hat. There are many varieties in shapes of women's hats, and with a knowledge of the general shapes it will not be difficult to turn any name into a hat of some kind. The script style such as "Alice" in Plate 27 is good to test the performer's imagination. Plate 28 shows six names using this style. The plain lettered style, such as "Frances" in Plate 27, is an even

PLATE 27
Evolution of Girls' Names

PLATE 28
Examples of Name Evolutions

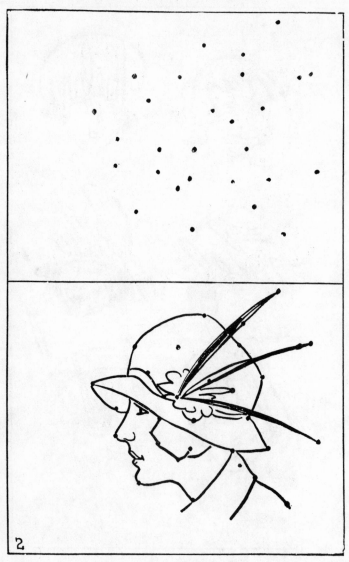

PLATE 29
A Pretty Girl Dot Picture

simpler way of handling the problem. Sit down and
try out about twenty-five names for practice, both in
script and in print. If a name should form an unusually funny shaped hat, finish the picture by making a comedy face under it.

DOT PICTURES.

Making dot pictures has the appearance of much
skill and dexterity and unusual thinking ability. In
reality it is not hard, and it becomes very simple and
easy of execution to the performer who tries it a few
times and who has a bit of imagination. The effect
is that someone from the audience puts a number of
heavy dots with black chalk on the white paper.
After this is done the performer, with a few lines,
connects the dots and forms a finished picture, of
which the dots form the foundation.

Plates 29 to 32 show how dots have been placed
hit or miss and pictures formed by connecting them.
No matter how complicated the arrangement of dots
may be the artist can almost always resort to a
woman's hat with a face peeking out beneath it.
The complicated shape of women's hats, with their
endless novelty of trimmings, is a valuable factor in
making dot pictures. Landscapes will also always
come to the rescue with the variety of clouds, trees,
hills, houses, ponds, brooks, roads, fences, etc. It
would be a wonderful series of dots that one could
not turn into a stone wall with trees behind it.

Here is the real secret of dot pictures: The audience thinks that the performer uses the dots as
points of a picture, when in reality he not only uses
them as points but he passes through them as well.
This process of passing through really amounts to

PLATE 30
A Comic Dot Picture

PLATE 31
A Novelty Dot Picture

PLATE 32
A Landscape Dot Picture

PLATE 33
A Snow Storm Dot Picture

PLATE 34
For the New Year

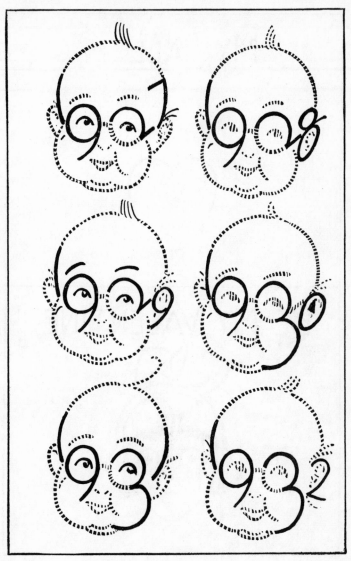

PLATE 35
Examples of Date Evolutions

MY ALL

BE MY VALENTINE

PLATE 36
For Valentine's Day

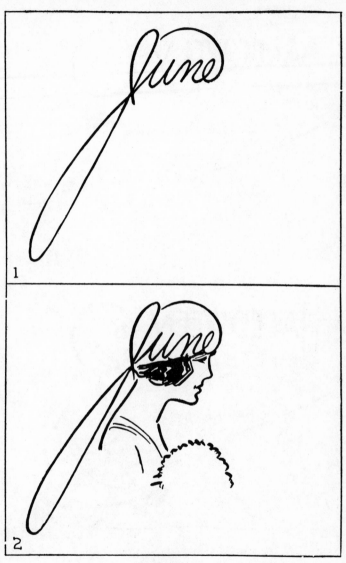

PLATE 37
For Orange Blossom Time

PLATE 38
For Hallowe'en

PLATE 39
For Thanksgiving Day

PLATE 40
For the Christmas Season

moving the dot to any point to fit the convenience of the artist.

Plate 33 shows an emergency way of handling dots by turning them into snowflakes. It is very seldom that a person puts a great quantity of dots on the paper but should anyone try to trip the performer by quantity production, this is a good way out of it.

SEASONABLE EVOLUTIONS.

As the various holidays and special seasons come along, timely novelties are in order, such as are suggested in Plates 34 to 40. The first stage of this kind of evolution drawing is often called the skeleton drawing. One charm of this style of work is that the skeleton lines appear to have been placed haphazard, without any special intention, and then suddenly, with a few added lines, they are converted into a finished picture.

In Plate 34 the date is easily transformed into a Happy New Year Kid. This shows how the numerals are converted into a baby's face, and how the skeleton lines are converted into a printed greeting by adding a few lines to complete the letters. Plate 35 shows how the same principle can be applied year after year by modifying slightly the face design.

In Plate 36 the Valentine spirit is introduced, and the season of the eternal June bride is the theme of Plate 37. A timely treatment of Hallowe'en is shown in Plate 38, and the time-honored Thanksgiving dinner is the basis of Plate 39. Plate 40 is a quickly made and sure-fire novelty for the Christmas season

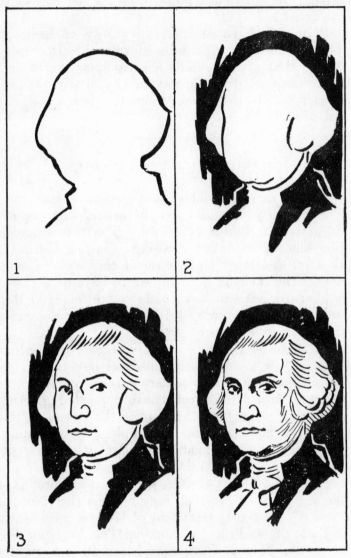

PLATE 41
George Washington

FAMOUS CHARACTERS.

Every locality has its popular idols and well-known characters whose likeness the chalk artist can readily utilize in many of his programs. There are many ways that portrait studies may be handled, depending largely on the skill of the artist. For ordinary purposes the rapid chalk portraits, simple in construction, are entirely serviceable. The pictures of George Washington (Plate 41) and Abraham Lincoln (Plate 42) are examples of this type of work. These plates show step by step how this kind of a picture is constructed, starting with a simple outline and finishing with the various shadows. Make portraits with black, brown, brick red or bright red crayon. These are the most popular colors for one-color work.

In reproducing a portrait in chalk get the best available photograph, drawing or painting of the person, study the outlines and shadows carefully and simplify the picture to its essential points, as has been done with the Washington and Lincoln pictures. Every person has certain outstanding characteristics in the construction of the head and face which, when carefully drawn and accented, emphasize the likeness.

Pleasing portrait work can be done by drawing on a medium toned paper such as gray, green, brown, blue, buff or sanguine. Draw the features and shadows in black or some dark color, and accent the high-lights and lighted features of the face and head in white, yellow or light flesh tone. This gives a three-color effect, the chalk serving for two colors and the paper a third.

The performer should, of course, ascertain the tone of local sentiment toward famous characters

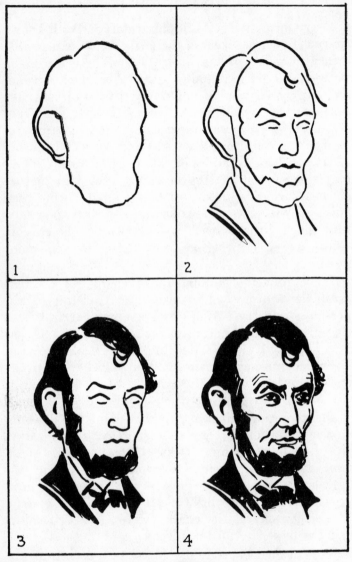

PLATE 42
Abraham Lincoln

before including them in his program. And he should indulge in comic caricatures only when he is sure that it will cause no resentment.

LANDSCAPES.

Landscape drawing is always popular. It affords a chance to awaken sentiment and create an atmosphere that either recalls pleasant memories or inspires happy thoughts of the future. It also furnishes a pleasant contrast to figures and novelty pictures. Landscapes can be drawn either with one color or with a variety. As a rule the latter pictures are made to reproduce as nearly as possible a color likeness to the real scene.

Scenic drawing with colors is not difficult if one has a fair idea of drawing and understands the principles of perspective and light and shade. The chalk talk performer who is not a natural artist and who is unable to work up original landscape ideas can easily find simple landscape pictures which he can copy or adapt for the purpose, if he wants to vary his program beyond the plates in this book.

The artist must strive for effect from the audience's standpoint. The coloring should be boldly handled, something in the style of the theatrical scene painter. Work which is rough when viewed close at hand blends in the distance into a smooth, apparently finely-drawn picture. It is wise to experiment freely, making a picture and then noting the effect some distance away.

Landscapes that are full of contrast, carry deep shadows and are high-lighted, win popular favor. The artist should strive for sharpness and snap in work of this kind. Many beautiful effects can be

PLATE 43
A Winter Scene in France

obtained by the proper application and blending of certain color combinations.

In beginning a picture the sky should be laid in first with color. This is done by using the flat side of the chalk. The rough marks are then smoothed over with a wad of cotton, or chalk. Or a good idea is to use the crayon in powder form, applying it with a good-sized powder puff. Powdered chalk blends nicely and covers well on large areas. Skies vary in color from sky-blue to the addition of gray for winter scenes or dull days, or to the addition of yellow, green, orange and red for sunrise, sunset, midday and moonlight. After finishing the sky, cover the ground part of the picture, which term includes both earth and water.

After the paper is thus well colored, gradually develop the more detailed work, leaving the finer details, deep shadows and high-lights until the last. The general rule is to work from the larger, broader surfaces in the background to the more detailed ones in the foreground. Thanks to the covering power of one color of chalk over another, details can always be put on last, regardless of what color is underneath.

Snow scenes are very effective. In Plate 43, a winter scene in France, the sky is drawn with sky-blue or gray-blue, laying the color on flat, nearly halfway down the sheet and not attempting to define the skyline. Then outline the left horizon and buildings with white, and cover all the blue below this outline with white, down to the bare paper. You now have the skyline sharply defined. The paper, being white, itself gives a snow effect for the foreground.

Stippled shading is used in the plate to represent the flat tones of brown that are next added to make the houses and the tracks down the road. The out-

PLATE 44
Florida Moonlight

PLATE 45
The Tiger

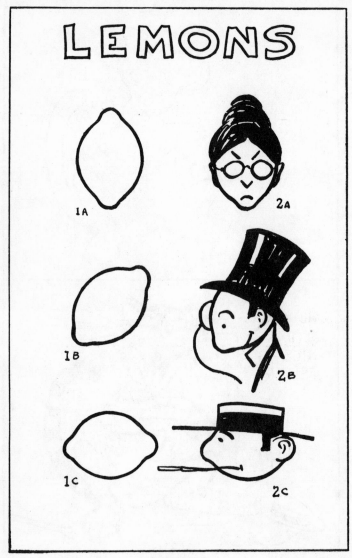

PLATE 46
A Few Lemons

PLATE 47
A Testimonial

Suggested Patter:

This is a portrait of
Miss Rhinoceros who won FIRST
prize at the Beauty Show on the
theory that if beauty is skin deep,
her thick skin must make her very
beautiful.

PLATE 48
The Prize Beauty

lines are then drawn with black. Color the two larger chimneys red. The evergreen trees are next put in with dark green and given a snow-laden effect with white chalk. White chalk should be used further to tone up any part of the picture where snow is needed, such as on the roofs and chimney tops.

The little old woman coming down the road with a bundle of firewood on her back is drawn last. The firewood should be brown, the dress dark blue and the cap and apron orange.

Plate 44 shows a Florida moonlight scene. The sky is ultramarine blue, which should be thoroughly smoothed with cotton. The water is green. The trees, foliage, house, boat and figures are drawn in black. The roof of the house is light yellow-brown. The light shining through the windows and door is orange with a touch of red. The moon is yellow, and the ripples of moonlight on the water are yellow or white. The light shining from the house should be the last thing drawn.

Musical accompaniment often adds considerably to the effect when drawing landscapes.

AN EXTRA COLOR EFFECT.

In many pictures the addition of an extra color greatly heightens the effect created. A flat tone here and there gives added brightness and snap. For instance in Plate 45 the tiger is much more effective if colored orange. In the beginning of this picture take a stick of orange chalk and draw in flat color the picture of the tiger (figure 1), silhouette style. Then take a stick of black chalk and draw the tiger on top of the silhouette background. This brings out the tiger in colors. The clothing on the ground

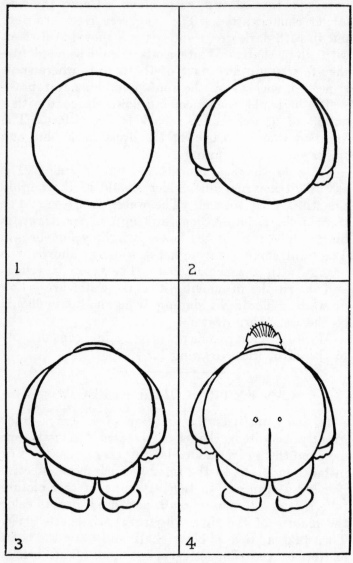

PLATE 49
The Fat Man

may be likewise colored, yellow for the hat and blue for the shirt.

In Plate 46 draw the silhouettes of three lemons with orange chalk. Yellow chalk does not show up very well at night. Then draw an outline in black around the orange silhouetted lemons. They are now ready for transformation with black chalk into the three characters as shown on the right-hand side of the plate.

THE FAT MAN.

This is an easy way to caricature a fat man. By drawing a rear view it eliminates the drawing of the face. In selecting a character to draw, note whether he is bald-headed, or has a peculiar style of hair cut, or wears a distinctive type of hat. In a picture of this kind the back of the head really identifies the person being caricatured. If the person has no special characteristic of the sort, the chalk artist can make an indirect remark which will help give the audience a clew, or if the man is in the audience the artist can stop once or twice and look at him as though in search of additional details for the drawing. Start with a circle and add the curved lines step by step as shown by figures 1, 2, 3 and 4 in Plate 49.

THE TALL MAN.

This is a good laugh getter, and an excellent picture for closing a short, snappy program. However, it fits well most anywhere in a program. The performer says he will draw the tallest man in the

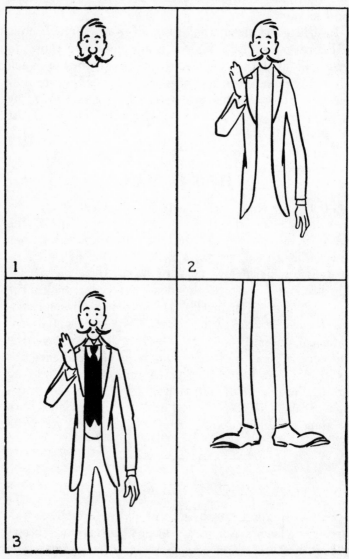

PLATE 50
The Tall Man

audience. Looking around he picks out as tall and thin a man as can be seen.

In drawing, start with the head and continue drawing until the knees reach the bottom of the page. Then take the paper off the board, turn it over, place it back on the board and finish the drawing on the other side. Of course the idea is that the man is so tall that one side of the paper isn't big enough to draw him on. See Plate 50.

In drawing the head and face make as good a caricature as possible.

TO GET A PERSON FROM THE AUDIENCE ON TO THE PLATFORM.

It may not seem difficult to get a member of the audience to come on to the platform when requested, for such purposes as making dots or putting marks of some other kind on the board. But it is nevertheless a hard problem at times, and sometimes an artist even has to eliminate certain pictures because it is impossible to induce anyone to act as a volunteer assistant.

When a spectator is asked to come on to the stage, a peculiar uneasiness, or species of stage fright, may come over him. He would like to comply, but he seems rooted to his seat. This can be overcome to a great extent by a proper method of approach and due use of the power of suggestion. A volunteer can be coaxed along in easy stages, so gradually that he is on the platform almost before he realizes it.

For instance, let us assume that the performer wishes to have a man come up on the stage to draw dots to be converted into a picture. If he asks point blank for a volunteer to do this, he may ask in vain. So instead he takes a piece of chalk and, going into the audience, he asks a man if he will kindly hold the chalk. His conversation may run about like this: "Thank you. Hold it just a little higher so that the gentleman back there can see it." No one, no matter how averse to appearing in public, is likely to refuse such a reasonable request. The performer continues, after glancing about. "I beg pardon, but a lady back there says she cannot see. Will you kindly stand up?" The assistant will in all probability stand up rather than make himself even more conspicuous by refusing. "Better yet, just step out into the aisle." By this time the assistant is more or less accustomed to being the center of attention, and often comes into the aisle with less hesitation than when he merely accepted the chalk. The proper gestures of suggestion are also invaluable. "Oh, yes, I did forget the people in the rear (or in the balcony). Will you just come up on the stage with me?" Taking the spectator's arm in a friendly manner the performer escorts him to the easel, giving him confidence and self-assurance in the same manner that a swimming teacher, by dispelling fear and with a reassuring touch of the hand when necessary, gets his student gradually into the deep water from the shallows.

When the suggestion is administered as above outlined, and the proper atmosphere of friendliness is established and maintained, very few people can refuse to comply.

Once the spectator has been induced to assist, the performer should not violate that confidence in the mistaken idea of creating comedy. An audience always likes to see an outsider on the platform and always hopes that something funny will happen while he is there. But if discourtesy is offered him the audience will resent it as a personal insult. The moment aversion is aroused, the performer has lost his grip on the audience and his effort to entertain is a failure.

In other words, the audience wants to laugh, but the comedy they enjoy is the kind that is unconsciously created by the visitor, not practical joking or "guying" at the assistant's expense. They may have a hearty laugh at an unconsciously awkward attitude of the assistant as he stands before the board to draw, or they may be amused at his being obviously ill at ease.

But the performer's attitude should be that of one who does everything in his power to make the volunteer assistant feel at home. He should maintain unbroken the bond of sympathy and friendliness, and let the comedy develop as it may from the actions of the assistant in a strange and unexpected environment.

LOCAL CARICATURES.

Audiences like to see pictures drawn of people whom they know personally, especially humorous caricatures. Such cartoons not only serve to reveal the skill of the artist, but the good-natured emphasizing of individual perculiarities in picture form is always a source of amusement. If the performer goes in for cartoons and caricatures he should investigate local interests and local happenings, and plan his pictures accordingly, for it is the local touch that makes the hit.

One general rule regarding caricatures is impor-

PLATE 51
A Closing Picture

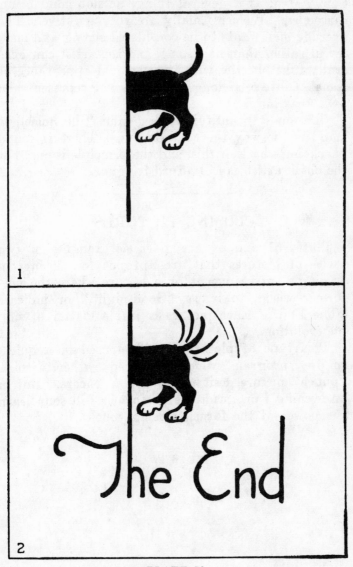

PLATE 52
Another Closing Picture

tant.   Men, as a general thing, do not mind being cartooned. Women usually are very sensitive. The average man wants to be considered strong and masterful rather than handsome, and the artist can generally take liberties with the personal appearance of a male subject, as long as he does not represent him as a weakling.

"The most beautiful woman" and "the homeliest man" is the way the contests run. There is sound psychology back of this, and the principle is one that the chalk artist can ill afford to ignore.

CLOSING PICTURES.

Plates 51 and 52 are given as examples of two styles of pictures that are apropos for closing an evening's entertainment or a lecture where the performer wishes to bid a "Good-night," or indicate "The End." Each picture is just a matter of simple evolution.

This type of picture is seldom used in a quick, snappy program, which is closed rather with a "punch" picture designed to get an encore. But in an evening's program the performer will soon learn the power of the formal closing touch.

Section II

FUN WITH CHALK TALK

HINTS ON CHALK TALKING

In the other chalk talk books of this series, the essential rules of chalk talking have been very well covered, but they cannot be driven home too hard, as they enable the artist to put over the chalk talk with greater power and punch and to give it the professional touch.

They are as follows:

1. Personality is important. Be alive and interested and put snap into your work. Develop ease and poise in working.

2. Make every line and every move count. Let the audience see what you are doing. The only places you need to cover up are the various secret features of the magical pictures. Then do your covering well. An important item in good showmanship is the use of great care in having spectators see clearly what you want them to see and drawing their attention away from what you do not want them to see.

3. To help develop confidence and smoothness in working, it is well for the artist to pencil the various subjects lightly on the paper—too lightly to be seen by the audience, yet heavily enough to be seen by the artist himself. Even the great artist working with pen and ink, water colors, or oil makes an advance layout with

pencil before putting on his ink or color. This outline acts as a guide for the deliberate strokes of the finished picture. The audience need not know of the preliminary lines. What they do not know will not hurt them. After all, it is results that you want, and the thing by which you are judged. Certain simple chalk pictures can be drawn without guide lines, but until you are well trained and sure of your ground, it is best to pencil the pictures in advance. This is particularly true in the trick pictures, which require proper location to create the various effects.

4.   Work from the side of the board as much as possible, so as not to screen the paper from the audience any more than necessary.

5.   After drawing a picture, pause a moment so that the audience will have plenty of time to catch the meaning of it. This pause, however, should not be too long. Also, pause a moment between any two changes or transformations in pictures.

6.   As each drawing is finished, lay it on the floor beside the easel or on a table, or hang it on another easel close at hand, which has two nails projecting from the top of it to hold papers.

7.   Be careful not to expose the backs of the magical pictures, as it is better to keep the audience mystified as to the manner in which they are made.

8.   Keep your act alive by putting plenty of variety into it. Act as though you enjoy your work, and talk

PLATE 4
The Vanishing Line

clearly and distinctly so that you can easily be heard in all parts of the house.

9.   Keep on the lookout for new ideas, better means of presentation, and opportunities to adapt pictures to local surroundings. A good-natured joke on some well-known local character often goes well.

10.   Rehearse every detail of the chalk talk before presenting a program, and use special care to keep it the right length. A long-drawn-out performance grows tiresome. Learn to stop drawing and close your program at the psychological moment, while the interest is still at its height. A chalk talk picture calls for speed and an apparently spontaneous enthusiasm.

11.   Whenever possible, have a musical accompaniment during the drawing of each picture, as music makes the chalk drawing easier and more agreeable to present.

12.   Plan your programs so that they will have dramatic value, continuity, variety, and snap. You will find enough suggestions and pictures in this book for many programs. Also, you can mix them with material from other sources to considerable advantage, notably with pictures from other books of this series.

MAGICAL CHALK DRAWINGS

These so-called magical chalk stunts will always hold a popular place on chalk talk programs, because of their element of surprise. They are so out of the usual run of chalk talk pictures. They are very simple to construct

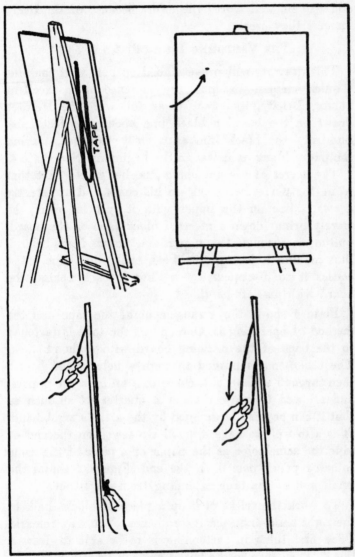

PLATE 5
The Vanishing Line (concluded)

and will be well worth the effort because of the lively interest they create.

THE VANISHING LINE (Plates 4, 5)

This drawing will prove a good opener, as it contains a quick surprise and puts the audience in an excellent humor. Briefly, its effect is as follows: The lecturer draws on the board a black line about two feet long. Suddenly the black line apparently vanishes, leaving the paper blank as it was in the beginning. See Plate 4.

The secret of the vanishing line lies in the fact that while the performer picks up his chalk and apparently draws a line on the paper with it, yet in reality he merely brings down a piece of black tape on the board, pulling it through the paper and board from behind, thus making it look quite like a chalk line. The artist causes it to disappear by pulling it back behind the board with his left hand.

Plate 5 shows the arrangement of the tape and the method of operating it. One end of the tape is fastened to the back of the drawing board with a thumb tack. The other end is pushed through a hole in the board, then through a small slit, cut with a knife in the papers, and allowed to project about a quarter of an inch so that it can be readily grasped by the artist's right hand. It is also well to have a small tip sewed on the end of tape the same color as the paper or a piece of the same color of paper pasted on the end. Figure 2 shows the small end of the tape extending from the paper.

To work the trick, pick up a piece of black chalk in the right hand and face the audience. You may remark, "The first thing in cartooning is to be able to draw a line." Then turn to the board and apparently place the crayon on the paper. What you really do is to grasp

PLATE 6
A Stylish Gentleman

the end of tape with the thumb and the first finger of the right hand, as in Figure 2, Plate 5. The left hand grasps the tape from behind the board, and pulls the tape down about two feet along the front of the paper, as in Figure 2, Plate 4 and Figure 3, Plate 5. Then turn your head toward the audience with the silent confirmation of the fact that you have done what you set out to do.

With your left hand, suddenly pull the tape back to the rear of the board, the right hand releasing it at the proper moment (Plates 4 and 5). The tape should be pulled clear of the board and the paper and allowed to hang down behind the board; and it should be short enough so that it will not dangle below the bottom of the board.

After the line has vanished, look at the paper in perplexity and then turn to the audience, saying, "As I said before, the first thing in cartooning is to be able to draw a line; but the next thing is to be able to keep it there."

A STYLISH GENTLEMAN (Plate 6)

The power of this picture lies in its surprise finish. The artist draws a colored gentleman in dress clothes and a monocle, then reaching into the upper left hand breast pocket of the gentleman's coat, he brings up a brightly colored red or green silk handkerchief and arranges it to complete the picture of a stylish figure.

To prepare for this effect, seal an envelope and cut off the top so that the opening will be at the top instead of at the side. Cut a slit in the paper, as shown in Figures 1 and 2, Plate 6, and on the back of the paper paste the envelope, opening upward, just below the slit in the paper. In the envelope place a brightly colored China

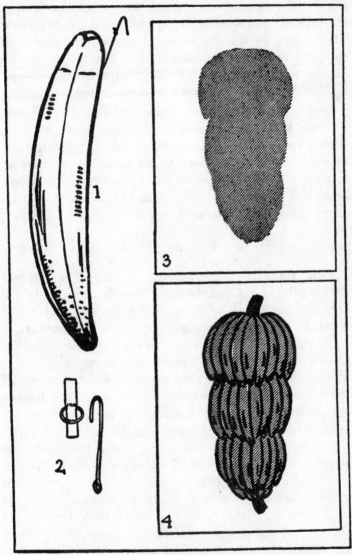

PLATE 7
Have a Banana

silk handkerchief about thirteen inches square. This is the type of handkerchief commonly used by magicians. The center of the handkerchief should be placed in envelope first and the corners last. On the front side of the paper lightly draw the figure of the colored gentleman so that the pocket will be in proper position.

In performing the trick, draw a picture as in Figure 3, Plate 6, adding the cord of the monocle at the finish —then turn to the audience as though the picture were finished. Finally turn back to the picture and, reaching through the slit in the paper and down into the envelope, bring out the corners of the silk handkerchief and arrange them, as in Figure 4.

Have a Banana (Plates 7, 8)

This stunt is a good laugh maker. The lecturer draws a bunch of bananas and then reaches up to the bunch and pulls off a banana, which he peels and out of which he takes a bite to show that it is a real banana.

To prepare for this picture, sew a stout piece of linen thread to the end of a banana, as shown in Figure 1, Plate 7, knot it well to keep in place, and to one end of the thread fasten a bent pin. Then place the banana thus prepared in your inside coat pocket or on the crayon tray beneath the drawing board out of sight. The pin is needed in order to pin the banana to the paper. Another method of attaching it is to have a small wire ring or clip fastened to the paper at the proper place with a small piece of gummed paper, as in Figure 2, Plate 7, with a metal hook tied to the thread instead of a pin. All that is necessary to fasten the banana is to hook it on the ring.

The stunt is performed as follows: With yellow cray-

PLATE 8
Have a Banana (concluded)

on draw the silhouette of a bunch of bananas (Fig. 3). With black crayon draw in the bananas (Fig. 4). While touching up the bananas at the right side, stand in front of the bunch long enough to take the real banana from your pocket and pin or hook it on the bunch at about the center of the middle row. Finish the drawing and turn to audience, then turn back to the board, reach up, and pull off the banana, as in Plate 8. You may remove a portion of the peel, take a bite, and toss the rest of the fruit to some one in the audience.

A Lemon While You Wait (Plates 9, 10)

Here is a surprise novelty that an audience always appreciates. The artist draws a lemon on the paper with yellow and black crayon. He places the crayon on the tray and reaches up and removes the lemon from the easel, leaving the paper blank. He holds up the lemon to convince his hearers that it is real and then tosses it to one of them (Plate 9).

After a careful study of Plate 10, it will be seen that Figures 1 and 2 show the front of the paper and Figure 3 the back. In Figures 1 and 2, it will be observed that one long slit has been cut vertically in the paper and two small slits have been cut diagonally. Through the large slit runs a strip of paper, which is held in place by inserting the ends in the diagonal slits. Figure 2 shows the approximate size in comparison with a real lemon. The drawing of the lemon is to be made on this strip.

Figure 3 shows the back of paper, on which is pasted an envelope, into which the strip of paper may be slid. To the strip a thread is attached and is run through a hole in the easel and tied to a wire letter clip. The clip

PLATE 9
A Lemon While You Wait

in turn is fastened to the edge of the drawing paper. When the clip is removed and the thread is pulled, the strip of paper disappears from the front of the drawing paper and goes into the envelope, carrying the pictured lemon with it and leaving the front of the paper blank. The real lemon should be concealed on the crayon tray.

The stunt is presented as follows:

With yellow or orange crayon, draw the lemon on the prepared strip of paper, outlining it with black crayon and shading it to look as natural as possible. Place the crayon on the tray and pick up the lemon in your right hand under cover of your body, holding it in the manner illustrated in Figure 4 and keeping the back of your hand toward the audience so that they cannot see the lemon concealed in it.

Plate 9 shows the method of inserting the lemon in the drawing. Bring the right hand, in which the lemon is concealed, in front of the pictured lemon, as in Figure 2, simultaneously removing the clip from the paper with the left hand and pulling the strip of paper into the envelope. Next, press the real lemon on the drawing paper and rest the right hand on the paper beneath it, so that it is exposed to the gaze of the audience. Then remove the lemon from the paper and hold it up to view, as in Figure 3. After convincing your hearers that it is a real lemon, you may toss it to one of the spectators.

The same paper used in this stunt may be prepared for another stunt immediately following it or may be utilized for drawing a regulation chalk talk picture. There is no good reason for removing a blank sheet of paper; so it should be used.

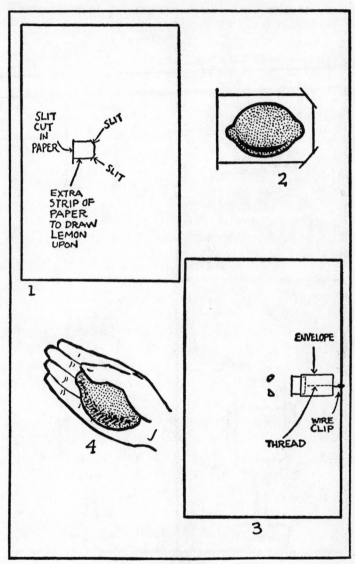

PLATE 10
A Lemon While You Wait (concluded)

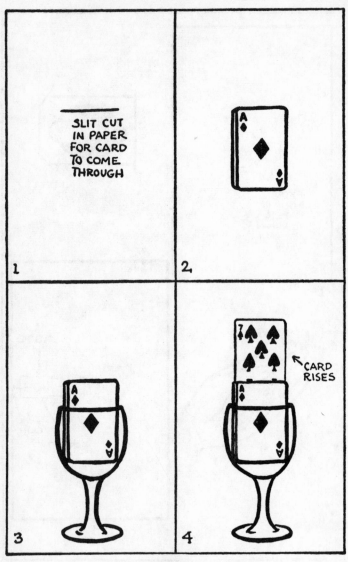

PLATE 11
The Rising Card

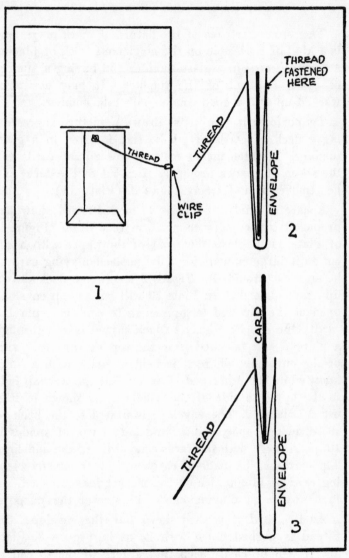

PLATE 12
The Rising Card (concluded)

The Rising Card (Plates 11, 12)

This stunt partakes of the nature of mock magic and is a kind of burlesque on the magician's trick of placing a deck of cards in a glass tumbler and having a number of cards rise out of the tumbler. It may easily be worked up into a good comic chalk talk number.

To perform it, the artist draws a picture representing a deck of cards of jumbo size inserted in a glass tumbler. He then makes motions toward the cards and the seven of spades promptly rises out of the deck, and he removes it and freely shows it (Plate 11).

A careful study of Plates 11 and 12 will show the preparation necessary to perform this stunt. Figure 1 of Plate 11 displays the front of the paper with a slit cut in it large enough for a large-sized playing card to be slipped through it. Figure 2 shows the deck drawn up against the slit. In Plate 12 will be seen an envelope open at the top and large enough to contain a playing card. One end of a coarse black thread is run through a pinhole and fastened near the top of the front side of the envelope, where it is held in place with a large knot, while the other end is passed through a small hole in the opposite side of the envelope, as shown in Figure 2, Plate 12. The envelope is pasted to the back of the drawing paper, and a handmade seven of spades is slipped into it, with the face turned toward the audience. The card may be made of cardboard stock, or any playing card of jumbo size on the market may be used. In fact, any large playing card will answer the purpose.

As the card is pushed down into the envelope, the thread is pushed down with it, as in Figure 3, Plate 12. It will be easily seen that a jerk of the thread at the back of the envelope will pull the card up out of

PLATE 13
The Honorable Mr. Donkey, Esq.

the envelope. The free end of the thread is tied to a metal letter clip and held in place on the edge of the paper, as in Figure 1, Plate 12.

In performing this stunt, first draw a picture of a deck of cards with black crayon, coloring the spots red and letting the top line cover the lower edge of the slit in the paper, as in Figure 2, Plate 11. Then draw a tumbler around the cards, as in Figure 3.

Then turn to the audience and inquire, "Pardon me, but what card did you say you selected?", addressing the query to some particular spectator. Before the latter has time to reply, answer your own question by saying, "The seven of spades. Thank you." Then turning and looking at the picture on the drawing board, take the clip from the side of the paper and say dramatically, "Seven of spades, arise!", at the same time pulling the thread.

This movement lifts the seven of spades out of the envelope, up through the slit, and, to all appearances, out of the pictured deck of cards. You remove the card and pass it around among the audience as proof of its genuineness.

The Honorable Mr. Donkey, Esq.
(Plates 13, 14, 15)

The donkey theme always lends itself readily to comedy. If, however, a few trick movements are assigned to the donkey, they intensify the comedy and bring out the element of surprise so necessary to good entertainment.

This donkey stunt contains all the elements of a comedy hit. A cartoon of a donkey is made on the drawing board. Suddenly he moves his eye around, looking here

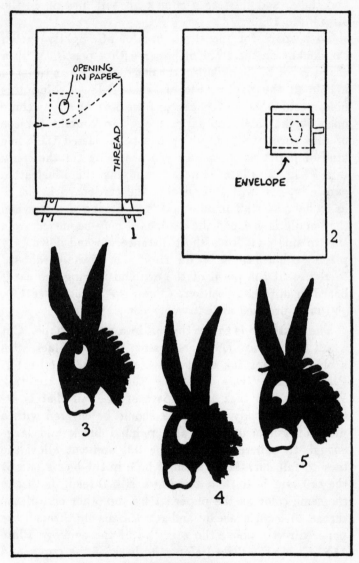

PLATE 14
The Honorable Mr. Donkey, Esq. (continued)

and there, and then as a climax his tail flies up in the air (Plate 13).

To prepare for the stunt, first of all, lightly sketch the donkey on the front of paper with a pencil. With a sharp razor blade or knife, cut out the eye so as to leave a hole in the paper (Fig. 1, Plate 14). Behind this hole, paste a sheet of paper to form sort of an envelope open at the sides and large enough to contain a piece of thin cardboard, on which has been pasted the same kind of paper as the paper you are using for the chalk talk (Fig. 2, Plate 14). By studying the illustration carefully, you will observe that the cardboard is cut so as to have a small handle and is so arranged that when the handle is grasped the cardboard may be moved from side to side and, for a short distance, up and down. By placing a black mark on the front side of the cardboard to represent the pupil of the eye and moving the cardboard in different positions (Figures 3, 4, 5, Plate 14), you may produce an extremely comical effect.

The next step is to get the tail into proper shape. Cut a tail out of cardboard and paint it a dead black with a black drawing ink or black water, japan, or oil color. Plate 15 effectively illustrates the shape of the tail. Place a thumb tack in the part of the tail that is attached to the body. This tack should be covered with a piece of gummed paper also painted black and large enough to adhere firmly to the tail and not allow the tack to fall out. Make a small hole in the bushy end of the tail and in it tie a fine black silk thread, or thread the same color as the paper. Pass the other end of the thread through a needle and run the needle through the paper directly above the rear end of the donkey (Plate 15). Carry the thread along the back of the paper and tie it to a wire letter clip, which is fastened on the edge

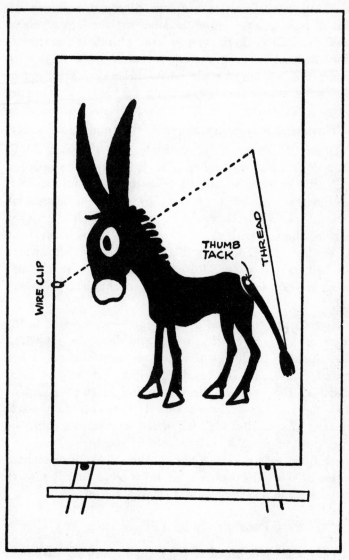

PLATE 15
The Honorable Mr. Donkey, Esq. (concluded)

of the paper. In Plate 15, the illustration shows the thread pulled taut—which is done just for sake of clearness. In reality, there is considerable slack to the thread, since it must be long enough to reach down to a point where the tail may be placed in the crayon tray out of the way, ready for the making of the chalk picture (Fig. 1, Plate 14).

This stunt may be presented in the following manner: Draw the donkey (Fig. 1, Plate 13), all but the tail. Step in front of donkey as though to draw the tail, but in reality merely pick it up from the tray and fasten it on the rear end of the donkey by means of the thumb tack (Plate 15). It would be well to touch the bushy part of the tail with the crayon as you draw away from it, so that the audience will think you have just drawn the tail on the paper. Be careful not to move the tail so as to expose prematurely any mechanical or tricky aid.

Step to the right side of the board—which side is the same as your right side when you face the audience. Bow slightly as though the picture were finished. Place your left hand on the handle projecting from the cardboard at the back of the paper and move it about so that the donkey looks backward, forward, downward, upward, diagonally, etc. Then remove the clip with the thread attached to it, or get hold of the thread and pull the tail up into the air (Fig. 2, Plate 13). The sudden whisk of the tail upward is so unexpected that it always surprises the audience into a hearty laugh.

The Pirate's Chest (Plates 16 to 19)

This stunt is a bit of novelty chalk drawing that puts an odd twist into the program. Into it could be worked

PLATE 16
The Pirate's Chest

a story of adventure dealing with pirates' gold and the discovery of a buried treasure chest. Stevenson's "Treasure Island" might be used as plot material on which to build a story. The artist might describe the burial of the chest and the return of the ghost of some victim, and then conjure up the spirit of the old pirate himself. A gong might be struck off stage several times when the ghost rises from the chest, and some sort of noise might be made when the pirate comes up. With the aid of a little imagination, the artist might work up an interesting chalk talk about the pirate's chest, the money, the ghost, and the pirate.

Briefly, the stunt works as follows: The artist draws a picture of a pirate's chest. He raises the lid of the chest and, reaching into it, lifts out a bag of money (Plate 16). Then from the chest, a ghostly figure slowly arises and sinks down into the chest again. Then the old pirate himself rises from the chest and finally disappears into it. The artist places the bag of money back in the chest and closes the lid, leaving the chest and its contents intact, as in the beginning.

In preparing for this stunt, make a light pencil drawing of the pirate's chest (Plate 17), and cut along the top edge of the chest with a sharp knife or razor blade so as to make a slit in the paper. Figure 1 shows the slit. The dotted lines represent the outline of an envelope on the back of the paper. Figure 2 shows the back of the paper with a large envelope pasted on it, the opening being at the top. The back of the envelope is cut down a little lower than the front in order to make pasting along the upper edge somewhat easier.

The drawings of the money bag, the ghost, and the pirate are cut out of cardboard and touched up with a

PLATE 17
The Pirate's Chest (continued)

brush dipped in black drawing ink. If the lecturer possesses real artistic ability, he may shade each picture to look quite natural by diluting the ink in water to various consistencies or by using water colors. Each drawing might even be made in colors to heighten the effect. The size of each figure will take a little experimenting, so that it may easily be concealed in the envelope beneath the slit cut in the paper.

The drawings of the ghost and the pirate are made to rise from the chest by means of a thread attached to each. In Plate 18, the thread arrangement is shown, using the ghost as an example. One end of the thread is attached to the ghost by the device of making a small hole near the top of his head, through which the thread is passed. A needle is threaded on the other end of the thread and run through the paper at a point directly above the center of the slit (Fig. 1, Plate 18). Then the needle is removed, and the end of the thread is tied to a wire letter clip fastened to the edge of the paper. Figure 2 shows the arrangement from the rear. By means of a tug on the thread, the ghost is pulled slowly out of the envelope to a position shown in Figure 3, Plate 16. As soon as the thread is slowly released, the ghostly figure slides down into the envelope again. The pirate is threaded in the same manner. A different sort of clip should be used for attaching the thread, so that the artist may easily see which controls the ghost and which governs the rising of the pirate.

The picture of the bag of money is deposited in the envelope in front of the drawings of the pirate and the ghost. A lid is cut from the same kind of paper as that used for the chalk work (Fig. 1, Plate 19). A thumb tack is placed in the lower left-hand corner. On the

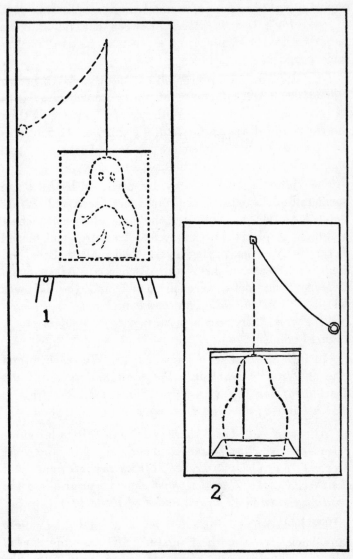

PLATE 18
The Pirate's Chest (continued)

opposite right-hand side, a small piece of chewing gum or conjuror's wax is placed between the lid and the paper to hold it in place; or a pin may be used for the same purpose.

This stunt may be presented as follows: With brown crayon draw the silhouette of the pirate's chest, with its lid (Fig. 2, Plate 19). With the black crayon outline the chest and draw in the details Figure 3. It may also be touched up with green crayon to indicate age, and high lights inserted with touches of orange.

The following patter may be used, with the stage business indicated: "Years ago there lived old Pirate Pete. Like all good pirates, he had a treasure chest in which he placed his money and treasures and buried it far away from prying eyes. Years after Pete had died, the treasure chest was discovered. After much difficulty, the locks were pried off and the lid was raised." *(Lift the lid. The thumb tack acts as a hinge, and the gum, wax, or pin permits it to be held in place, as in Figure 4.)*

"Inside the chest were bags of gold. We reach in and take out one." *(Reach into the chest and take out the drawing of the bag of money. Place it on the tray so that it leans against the drawing paper.)*

"All was well until there was suddenly a peculiar noise—an unearthly sound—and suddenly from the chest a ghostly figure slowly arose." *(With the left hand, pull the thread controlling the ghost slowly upward into the position shown in Figures 2 and 3 of Plate 16.)*

"He looked about for a few moments and then slowly sank back into the chest again." *(Release the thread slowly, allowing the ghost to slide back into the envelope.)*

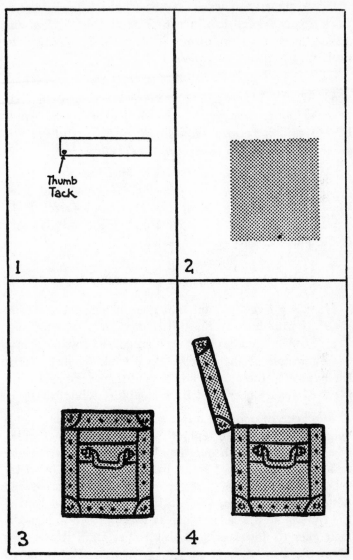

PLATE 19
The Pirate's Chest (concluded)

"Then from the chest another figure slowly arose. Look! It is the spirit of Pirate Pete himself." *(Pull the thread controlling the pirate, lifting him up slowly into position, as shown in Figure 4, Plate 16.)*

"It is old Pirate Pete, who roamed the seas so long ago. Slowly he, too, goes back into the chest he has haunted for so many years, where his earthly treasures lie buried." *(Release the thread slowly, allowing the pirate to sink slowly back into the envelope.)*

"We will put the money back into the chest again *(place bag of money back into the envelope)*, and close the lid." *(Close the lid of the chest and fasten it in position.)* "And we will leave Pirate Pete and his chest of treasures as they were."

A Drink to Order (Plates 20, 21)

Here is a comedy stunt that goes well in these piping times of prohibition. The artist draws the picture of a keg of beer. Then picking up a spigot, he inserts it into the bung hole of the barrel, takes drinking glass, turns the handle of the spigot, and proceeds to draw himself a glass of foamy beer, which he samples (Plate 20).

The beer, which is really near beer, is contained in a specially constructed spigot made out of a regular wooden spigot, which may be obtained at a hardware or a department store. To the back end is fitted a metal tube (Fig. 1, Plate 21), the rear end of which is covered with a screw cap or close-fitting cork. In the top of the tube is an air hole, which is necessary to induce the near beer to flow freely at the proper time. Until that time, the hole is kept sealed by means of a layer of wax or gum. It is sometimes advisable to paste a cover-

PLATE 20
A Drink to Order

ing of paper also over the hole beneath the wax or gum, to prevent the clogging of the hole when the wax is lifted off. If preferred, a small wooden peg may be inserted in the air hole and pulled out when it is time to start the flow of near beer from the spigot.

In filling the spigot, be sure that it is closed. Open a bottle of near beer carefully and pour it into the back end of the tube. Do not stir up the liquid any more than is necessary, since it is later supposed to foam. When the tube is almost full of the liquid, put the cork or screw cap into the end of the tube. Figures 2 and 3 of Plate 21 show a type of screw cap used with great success. It has a slit in its top that is turned by inserting a coin into it, as in Figure 2.

Cut two slits in the paper crossing one another (Fig. 4). These slits must pass through all the other papers on the drawing board back of this one, and in the board itself must be cut a hole large enough to hold the tube of the spigot comfortably. When the spigot is apparently pushed into the bung hole of the barrel, it is really pushed through the papers and the hole in the board. It should be held tightly enough so that you can easily manipulate the spigot and allow the near beer to run out into a glass held beneath it. The most convenient type of glass to use is a stein that holds very little liquid.

In presenting this stunt, draw the silhouette of the keg in brown, outline it with black, and fill it in to represent a beer keg (Fig. 5, Plate 21). Pick up the spigot, removing the gum or the wax or the wooden plug, so as to admit the air. Push the back end of the spigot into the bung hole of the barrel, pick up the stein, and hold it under the spigot. Turn the handle and let the beer run into the glass, turning it off when enough near

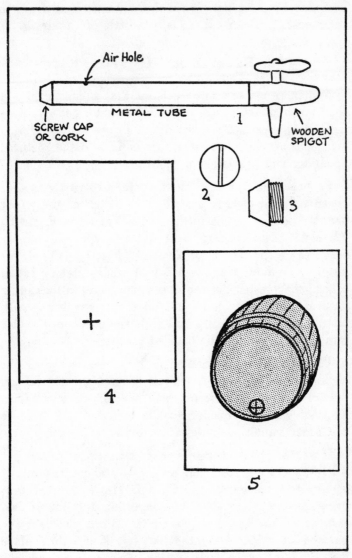

Air Hole

METAL TUBE   1

SCREW CAP
OR CORK

WOODEN
SPIGOT

2

3

4

5

PLATE 21
A Drink to Order (concluded)

beer has been let out. Face the audience and drink to their health. You need sip only a little of the drink.

THE RABBIT IN THE HAT (Plate 22)

Audiences always enjoy a stunt that suggests the old familiar magician's trick of taking a rabbit out of a plug hat. In this case, the artist draws a picture of the plug hat, then apparently reaches his hand into the pictured headgear and draws out a rabbit.

Preparations for this stunt again involve the use of an envelope, which is pasted on the back of the paper directly beneath a slit in the paper, cut as in Figure 2, Plate 22. The opening is at the top. On white cardboard draw the picture of a rabbit (Fig. 1). The drawing may be done with black ink or with water or japan colors, with which the rabbit may be made to look quite natural. Next, cut the rabbit out of the cardboard with scissors or a sharp knife and slide the cardboard rabbit into the envelope on the back of the paper (Fig. 2).

The stunt is performed as follows: Draw a plug hat on the paper with black crayon (Fig. 3), with the top line of the hat coinciding with the slit in the paper. Through the slit, reach into the hat and take out the cardboard rabbit, holding it up to the audience

If you wish to produce a more sensational effect, get a live rabbit and put him into a box about ten inches square with an opening at the top. Have your assistant bring to the stage the box containing the rabbit and stand near the board at your left. When you take the pasteboard rabbit from the hat, lift it up, then place it in the box your assistant holds. Then turn to audience and say, "Oh, you want to see him closer?" Lift out the

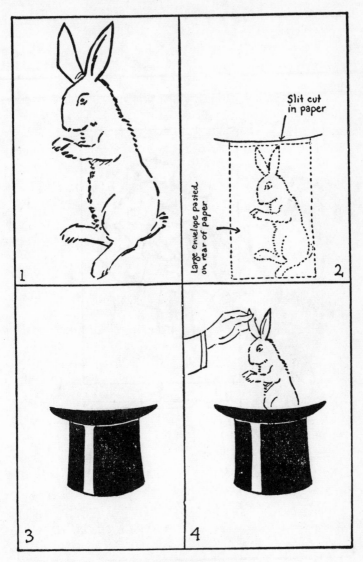

Slit cut in paper

Large envelope pasted on rear of paper

PLATE 22
The Rabbit in the Hat

PLATE 23
An Easy Way to Make Money

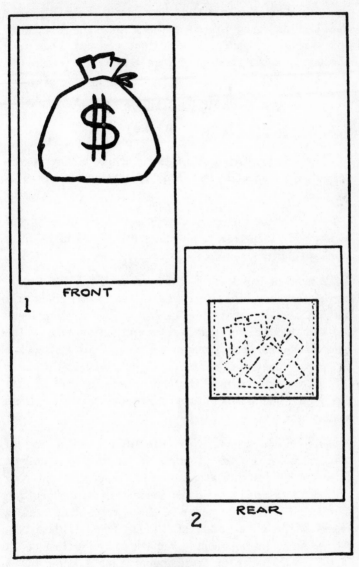

PLATE 24
An Easy Way to Make Money (concluded)

live rabbit by the ears and show him to be really alive and kicking, then drop him back into the assistant's box. Whatever color of live rabbit you use, have your cardboard rabbit match him as closely as possible.

An Easy Way to Make Money
(Plates, 23, 24)

There is always popular interest where money in concerned and especially when it is obtained by pseudo-magical means.

In this stunt the artist draws a picture of a bag of money. He then tears a hole in the bag and takes out a stack of bills.

To present this trick picture, you will require a number of currency bills, in addition to the usual chalk talk materials. To prepare for the stunt, glue a rather large sheet of paper along its two sides and bottom edge to the back of the chalk talk paper (Fig. 2, Plate 24). Thus the paper makes a kind of envelope glued to the chalk talk paper and open at the top. Place the roll of currency bills inside this improvised envelope, packing them as flat as possible.

With black crayon draw the picture of a bag of money, as in Figure 1, Plate 24, remarking, as you finish it, "There you are, money!" Then take out your pocket knife and with it slit the bag crosswise, cutting it open. Tear off the paper of the envelope underneath, take out the bills, and exhibit them freely (Plate 23). At the same time, you may remark to the audience, "It is the easiest way to make money that I know of. I draw my own salary."

PLATE 25
The Eternal Question

NOVELTY CHALK TALKS

We will leave the magical chalk pictures and take up
a department of chalk talking which does not require
previous preparation, though the climax of each picture
comes from the drawing itself. The changing of one
picture into another, step by step, has always been popular with audiences. In the following pages is given a
good selection of novelty transformation chalk talks,
with suggestions for patter.

The Eternal Question (Plate 25)

This plate shows how a question mark may be transformed into a woman's head by a few additional lines.
First of all, draw the question mark to cover a considerable part of the sheet of paper. Turn to audience and
say, "This is the question—the ordinary question." Now
add the line as in Figure 2 and finish with the face,
as in Figure 3. Then add to the audience, "But this is
the eternal question."

The Rising Sun (Plates 26, 27)

For this picture, first draw the round ring of the sun
itself, then the rays projecting outward. Under the sun
draw the outline of a mountain top. Underneath it, in-
scribe the words, "The Rising Sun." You do not need
to talk in connection with the drawing of this picture,
since the lettering tells the story. However, to emphasize the idea, you may at this point turn to the audience
and say, "The rising sun."

Turn to the board again and quickly draw the face,
the figure, the bed, and the alarm clock shown in Plate

PLATE 26
The Rising Sun

PLATE 27
The Rising Sun (concluded)

PLATE 28
Paul Revere's Ride

27, and finish by changing the *u* in "sun" to *o*. This change at the finish gives the picture its final punch.

PAUL REVERE'S RIDE (Plates, 28, 29)

The artist draws a picture to represent the Revolutionary patriot, Paul Revere, in action (Plate 28).

Turning to the audience he says, "What was it that Paul Revere said at the end of his famous midnight ride? What immortal saying has he handed down to the future generations? Listen, my children and you shall hear. At the end of his famous midnight ride he said, 'Whoa!'"

As you speak the word, "whoa," letter it in quickly. The action and the word should be well synchronized.

MONEY OR LOVE (Plates 30, 31)

The artist draws a picture of a bag of money at upper left side of the paper, as in Plate 30, and then sketches the heart at the lower right side, addressing the audience as follows:

"To marry or not to marry is the question. And if you do marry, whom shall you marry? For what shall you marry? Money or love?"

(Draw the face and change the money bag into the girl's head, as in Plate 31.) "She has money."

(Change the heart into the girl's head as in lower figure of Plate 31.) "And she has love. The answer, my friends, is: Be rich yourself and pick whom you please."

HIP, HIP, HOORAY! (Plate 32)

Here is a picture with considerable action. It is one of those foolish stunts that audiences welcome now and then.

PLATE 29
Paul Revere's Ride (concluded)

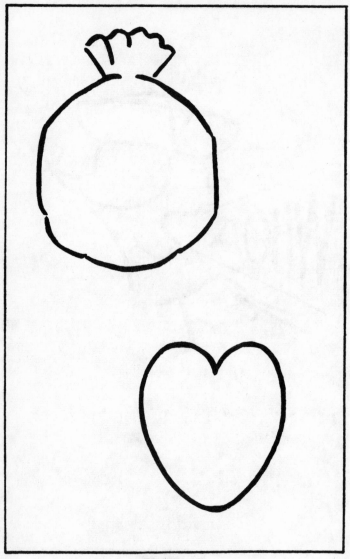

PLATE 30
Money or Love

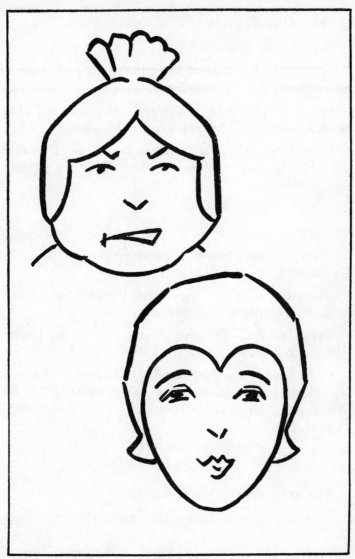

PLATE 31
Money or Love (concluded)

The artist draws one chair, as in Figure 1, then says to the audience:

"Cheer up. One cheer."

(Draw another chair at the right of the first chair, as as in Figure 3.) "Three cheers."

(Draw a third chair at the right of the second chair as in Figure 3.) "Three cheers."

(For the finish, quickly letter in the words "Hip, Hip, Hooray," the chairs taking the place of the H's.) "Hip, hip, hooray!"

Brain Food (Plate 33)

Plate 33 shows how a fish may be changed to a man by the addition of a few lines.

The artist draws the fish, which should be of a fairly large size, saying to the audience:

"This is a fish. They say that a fish is very brainy. He goes nutty over a couple of worms."

(Add lines to the fish, sketching the face of the man, as well as his hat, as in the lower picture of Plate 33. When the picture is finished, turn to the audience.) "Brain food."

Zulu Zu (Plate 34)

The artist says to the audience:

"Let us take a trip to Zulu Land, where the Zulus live."

(Draw the two huts and the palm tree, as in Figure 1, Plate 34.) "Two little houses, side by side; and a

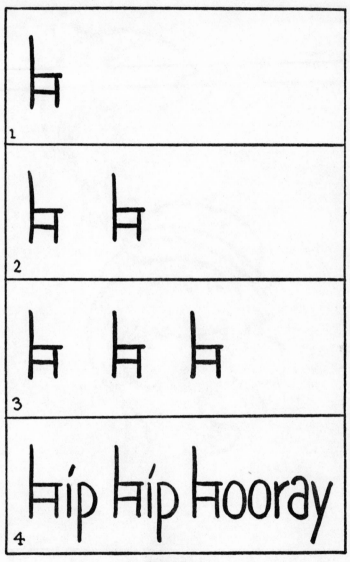

PLATE 32
Hip, Hip, Hooray!

PLATE 33
Brain Food

PLATE 34
Zulu Zu

bending palm that grows outside. Oh, where is my wandering boy to-night?"

(Draw the upper semicircular line from the top of the tree, shown in Figure 2.) "Ah, a rainbow."

(Then draw the nose, as in Figure 2.) "A glimmering pool."

(Complete the outlines of the Zulu's head, as in Figure 3. Then fill in the head with black crayon, adding the hair and the earrings, and widening the mouth at the finish, as in Figure 4.) "Old Zulu Zu himself!"

If desired, the earrings may be drawn with orange or red crayon—which will add to the striking effect of the picture.

How a General Is Made (Plate 35)

The artist draws the picture of two soldiers talking to each other, as in Figure 1, Plate 35.

Then he says to the audience:

"Aha! Two soldier boys—Spanish, Mexican, Nicaraguan, or South American. What are they talking about? They have army news. What is army news? You have to be in the army to know what army news is; even then you do not know. It is made to order while you wait. But there is usually one thing certain, and that is, you must give it the opposite interpretation in order to get the facts. The more you hear the less you know. The more you hear, the more it grows."

(Draw lines as in Figure 2 and Figure 3 and finally finish as in Figure 4.)

"Who is this? This is General Fuzzyface. How did he get to be a general? He said nothing, he heard

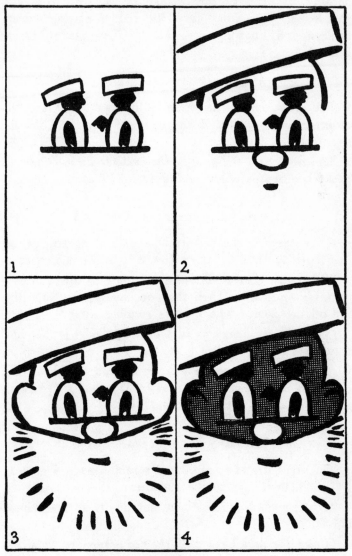

PLATE 35
How a General Is Made

nothing, he knew no gossip, and he gave no tips. He just looked wise. They gave him credit for being a deep thinker and knowing something. They made him a general!"

A Love Letter (Plate 36)

The artist draws the letter as in Figure 1, Plate 36, covering a good part of the sheet of paper. Then he says to the audience:

"A love letter." (*Draw in the outlines as in Figure 2 and fill in and finish, as in Figure 3.*) "And its results."

A Pair of Spectacles (Plate 37)

After drawing the picture of a pair of spectacles, as in Figure 1, Plate 37, the artist says to the audience:

"What are these? These are a pair of spectacles— women's spectacles. Are they on the lady? No, they are on the floor. The lady is running away."

(*Draw in the heads, as in Figure 2*) "Why is the lady running away?"

(*Remove the paper from the board and turn it upside down, showing the two mice, as in Figure 3.*) "There is a reason; in fact there are two of them."

The Red Rabbit (Plate 38)

The artist draws an outline of a rabbit, as in Figure 1, Plate 38, then says to the audience:

"White rabbits are common, but this is an uncommon one."

(*Color the rabbit red with the red crayon.*) "This is a red rabbit. He may be an Easter rabbit."

PLATE 36
A Love Letter

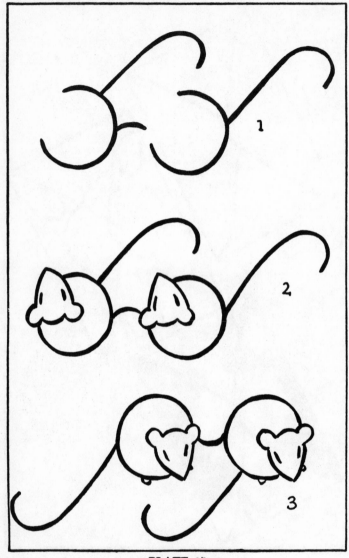

PLATE 37
A Pair of Spectacles

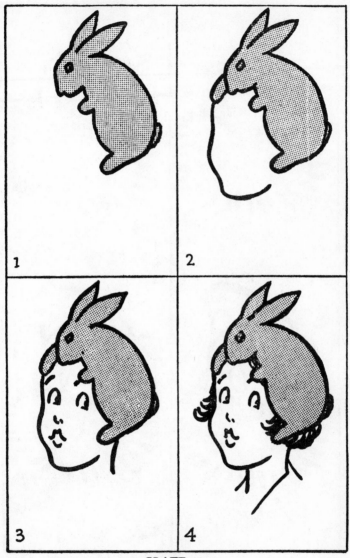

PLATE 38
The Red Rabbit

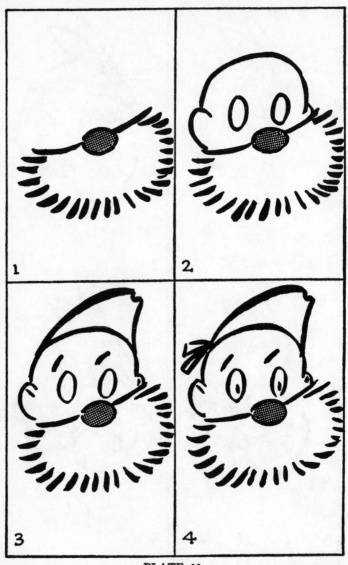

PLATE 39
The Scotchman's Hat

GREETINGS

I Wish You a Happy
Christmas
New Years
Valentine's Day
Easter
Fourth of July
Halloween
Thanksgiving
Wedding Anniversary
and Birthday
for the Years
1930 - 1931 - 1932
1933 - 1934 - 1935

PLATE 40
The Scotchman's Greeting Card

(Draw the left foot sticking out, as in Figure 2.) "He is sticking out his left foot. Whom is he waving at?"

(Continue as in Figures 2 and 3 and finish as in Figure 4.) "He is waving at one of his girl friends—the **girl** with the little red hat."

The Scotchman's Hat (Plate 39)

The artist draws the Scotch hat, as in Figure 1, Plate 39, making the button in red. Then he says to the audience:

"What have we now? A Scotchman's winter hat—button and all. To whom does it belong? **To Sandy McGee.**"

(Continue the drawing as in Figures 2 and 3.) "Is Sandy thrifty. Is he economical? Is he? Oh, boy!"

(Finish the picture in the manner indicated in Figure 4.) "He sticks up his hat and has a red nose without drinking, and never harvests his whiskers!"

The Scotchman's Greeting Card (Plate 40)

This chalk talk drawing speaks for itself. The artist merely makes the announcement, and the drawing of it step by step does the rest, with the final punch on the end. The lettering should be done as rapidly as possible. It is well to have penciled guide lines drawn lightly in pencil for the top and the bottom of the small letters. Guide lines help to keep lines of lettering fairly straight when the artist is working rapidly.

After making the announcement, "A Scotchman's greeting card," letter the word, "Greetings," with red crayon and underscore it with green or blue. The rest of the card may be lettered in black, with the exception

PLATE 41
The Pumpkin and the Witch

of the years, which should be done in red to emphasize the finish. Rightly presented, this stunt creates a strongly comic effect.

The Pumpkin and the Witch (Plate 41)

This chalk talk transformation is especially good for Halloween and autumn entertainments.

The artist draws the pumpkin in silhouette with orange crayon and finishes it up with black, then says to the audience:

"You have heard of the old lady who lived in a shoe. But did you hear of the old lady who lived in a pumpkin?"

(Continue drawing as in Figure 2 and finish by drawing the witch shown in Figure 3.) "This is the pumpkin witch herself."

The Darky and the Ghost (Plate 42)

The artist draws a picture of the ghost, then puts in the X with the broken line projecting upward and out to the side of paper. Then he says to the audience, "This is a picture of a darky shaking hands with a ghost."

Lines That Count (Plates 43 to 46)

This chalk talk is an interesting study in drawing, as it goes to show the importance of each line used in the making of a cartoon and keeps the curiosity aroused to the finish; for the audience keeps wondering what will happen next. One of the main essentials of cartoon drawing is to make every line count—to be able to tell a story in a nutshell. Each line tells its story in the

PLATE 42
The Darky and the Ghost

making of facial expression. So watch the effect, step by step, as every line is drawn.

To aid in simplifying the drawing, it is advisable to pencil in lightly the finished figure of the clown (Fig. 16, Plate 46). With the pencil lines as a guide, you can place each line with more care, more confidence, and a feeling of greater ease and allow yourself more concentration on the presentation and showmanship than if you worked without guide lines.

Begin by drawing the profile as shown in Figure 1, Plate 43. The slant of the eye and the eyebrow gives the profile an oriental or Chinese expression. With the addition of the cheek line in Figure 2, the face is given the hint of a smile. In Figure 3, the back of the head is added, while in Figure 4, by the addition of lines in the face, the figure changes from the profile of an oriental to the front view of a Caucasian.

Note what a change in the lines of the mouth will do, as shown in Figure 5, Plate 44, and the effect of opening the mouth in Figure 6. In Figure 7, the pupils are added to the eyes, while in Figure 8, the eyes are enlarged by means of lines underneath. Draw a mustache, as in Figure 9, Plate 45, and then the cheek lines, as in Figure 10, which place a smile on the countenance. The building up of the nose in Figure 11 changes the expression again, and the addition of the side lines on the eyes in Figure 12 increases the humorous expression.

It is interesting to observe how comedy is created, step by step, and how each line added contributes to the broadening of the smile and the general expression of happiness. Draw a line through the pupil of each eye and line in the ears, as in Figure 13, Plate 46, then add lines to the forehead, as in Figure 14, and finish up

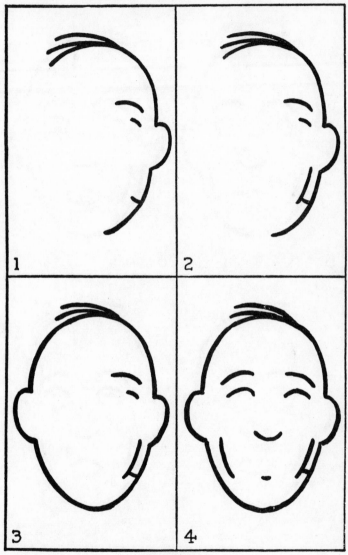

PLATE 43
Lines That Count

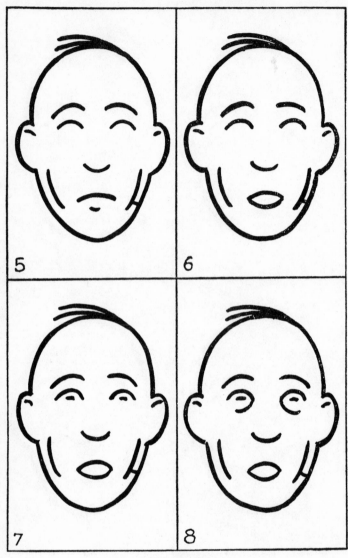

PLATE 44
Lines That Count (continued)

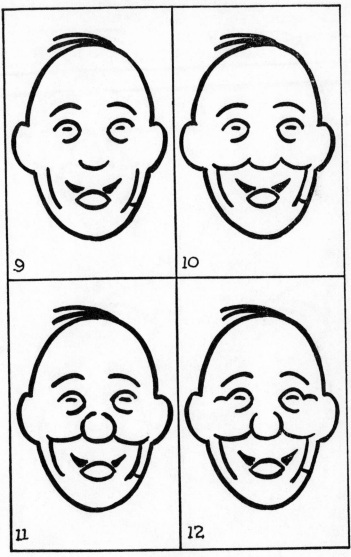

PLATE 45
Lines That Count (continued)

PLATE 46
Lines That Count (concluded)

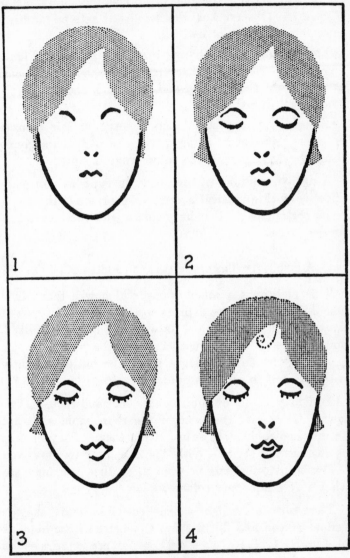

PLATE 47
A Study in Transformation

the mouth. Even the hat heightens the effect, as in Figure 15. Observe how the hair itself acts as the basic lines for forming the hat.

Finally finish by sketching the clown shown in Figure 16. The special lines characteristic of the clown, such as eyebrows, cheek lines, and chin line, show up well, when done in red.

Building up a picture step by step in this manner enhances your credit as an artist with audiences, giving them the feeling that you know your business.

A transformation picture of this type is unusually effective with a musical accompaniment, since the music has a certain swing that harmonizes with the movements of the artist.

A Study in Transformation (Plates 47, 48)

This picture is another example of how a touch here and there may change expressions of faces and types of figures.   This time, colors as well as lines are utilized, and a woman's head is used instead of a man's. In this case also, the finished figure should be outlined lightly with a pencil to serve as guide lines.

You may begin by addressing your audience as follows: "It is said that women are changeable and that no one knows what to expect from them. They change as fast as the styles. With chalk I want to show you a few transformations in woman, so that you may see what a few lines and colors will do."

Then turn to the lightly penciled guide lines, take the yellow crayon and fill in a flat silhouette of the hair, as in Figure 1, Plate 47. With black crayon draw the outline of the eyes, nose, and mouth. With yellow crayon

PLATE 48
A Study in Transformation (concluded)

extend the hair at the sides of the head a little, and with a black crayon add the drooping eyelids and the lower lip, as in Figure 2. In Figure 3 add eyelashes to the eyelids and give more accent to the mouth. In Figure 4, vary the coiffure by coloring the hair orange and having a curl on the forehead. Also, add a small line to the center of the mouth.

It will be observed that the expression changes considerably in Figure 5, Plate 48. Color the hair red, give the ends an upward twist at the sides of the head, and add black pupils to the eyes, shaded by eyebrows. For the next change, recorded in Figure 6, draw a black line through the eye just above the pupil, to serve as the upper eyelid, touch up the mouth, and with brown crayon color the hair, extending its area at the sides of the head. Finally, outline the brown area with black crayon, as in Figure 7, and fill it in entirely in black, as in Figure 8, in which you have the completed picture of a woman wearing a hat.

MEN WHO HAVE NEVER BEEN PRESIDENT
(Plates 49 to 52)

The title itself tells a good story, especially after one sees the figures drawn to illustrate it. Each figure calls for a short paragraph of patter to bring out the humor and present a clear portrait of each character sketched. The artist may draw two figures to a sheet of paper in the manner followed in the four plates, starting with the upper figure and finishing with the bottom one on each paper.

The artist thus addresses the audience:

"It is the custom for a cartoonist to draw men who have been President of the United States. Washington

PLATE 49
Men Who Have Never Been President

and Lincoln have always been popular, as well as Theodore Roosevelt or————." *(Mention the President in office at the time of drawing.)* "However, it is no more than right that we approach the subject from an opposite angle and present to you a number of men who have never been President."

(Turn to the board and draw the gentleman as shown in Figure 1, Plate 49.) "This is Mr. Squibbles, whose father's name was also Squibbles. Mr. Squibbles is an expert on the subject of peanut culture in a peanut-roasting machine and recommends the purchase of ten-cent packs of peanuts in preference to the customary five-cent purchases. Of recent years, Mr. Squibbles has added an attachment to the top of his machine for the sale of six varieties of chewing gum."

(Next draw the dude type illustrated in Figure 2.) "Allow me to present another gentleman who has never been President. This is Algernon Notweight. Algernon thinks that Indians inhabit the territory outside the city limits. He can close his left eye and see out of his right eye through his glass monocle very distinctly. In fact, he can look through his glass window and say, 'Bah Jove!' at the same time. He is his mother's idol. There is no doubt about his being idle."

(Sketch the old soldier of Figure 3, Plate 50.) "Well, well, if here isn't old Grandpa Fizzblossom himself! According to grandpa, he was quite a hero in the Civil War, and he often explains how he was the man in back of General Grant. Just how far back is not exactly known; in fact, it is alleged that when General Grant went eastward into battle, grandpa went westward. However, grandpa is always willing to have a drink,

PLATE 50
Men Who Have Never Been President (continued)

PLATE 51
Men Who Have Never Been President (continued)

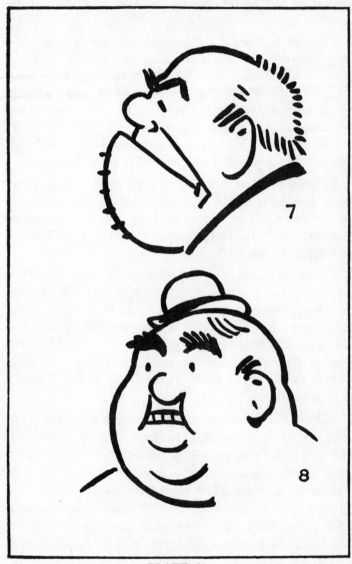

PLATE 52
Men Who Have Never Been President (concluded)

providing the water content of the drink is not too great."

(Figure 4, Plate 50, illustrates another type of character. Draw the hat first, then the head.) "This is Ezra Bullhummer. Ezra moved pianos for four years before he discovered that music could be made with the black keys as well as the white. Ezra is a very great advocate of noon and six o'clock whistles that blow loudly enough. Many a day Ezra stops an hour before the whistle blows, to make sure that he will hear it."

(Figure 5, Plate 51, gives a little variety by presenting a rear view of the subject.) "This is the usual view of Ambrose Whistlelotta as seen by bill collectors, charity collectors, and his wife on wash day. Ambrose is usually in retreat."

(Draw the picture of a janitor type, Figure 6, Plate 51.) "Ole has his own ideas on janitoring. He believes in having everything in season—cold in winter and hot in summer. Far be it from him to interfere with nature and keep the furnace fired in the winter and the refrigerators working in the summer! Ole brought his pipe over from the old country. It has been handed down for four generations."

(Draw the heavy-jawed gentleman in Figure 7, Plate 52.) "Behold Dynamite Mulligan. Little would you think that he was christened under the name of Aloysius. Dynamite has been a great student of the jail system in America. His records speak for themselves. He has his own favorite tests for liquor. He rubs some of it on a chair, and if the paint does not come off or the chair fall to pieces, he knows that it is good liquor."

(The last character to be drawn is the robust gentle-

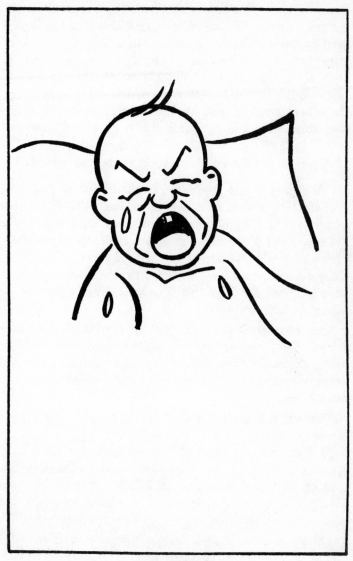

PLATE 53
The Old Family All-bum

man in Figure 8, Plate 52.) "And last but not least, is
our good friend, Elmer Warthogg. Elmer has served a
good purpose in his community. He is a great student of
relaxation, and by sitting in one spot most of the day,
he enables the other inhabitants of the community to
carry on their work unmolested. When Elmer was a boy,
the other boys did not have to waste money on comic
valentines. They merely sent Elmer around in person."

The Old Family All-bum (Plates 53 to 60)

Old family album stunts are popular because they give
a chalk talk artist a chance to utilize local characters
in an easy and humorous way without obliging him to
draw a good likeness. Portrait work and the carica-
turing of portrait features are not easy branches of art.
They require considerable study, practice, and a knowledge of good drawing. So it is well for no one but an
expert to attempt them.

The character portraits herein suggested for well-
known local characters will appeal to the chalk talk
artist because of the ease of their presentation and the
large proportion of comedy which may be extracted
from them.

The artist thus addresses the audience, as he plies
his crayon:

"I have always enjoyed looking over the old family
all-bum and seeing not only the pictures of to-day but
also of the days gone by. In looking over the all-bum
to-day, I examined with much interest some of the
pictures I am going to copy and draw for you to-night."

(Draw a picture of a baby crying, as in Plate 53.)
"This is ———— *(name of local character)* when he
was a baby. He had great possibilities of becoming

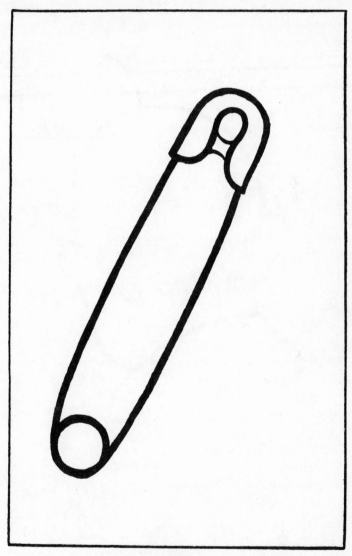

PLATE 54
The Old Family All-bum (continued)

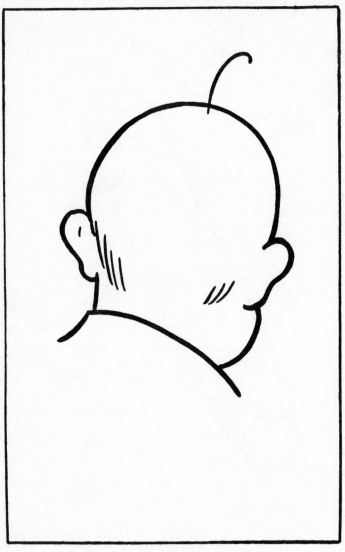

PLATE 55
The Old Family All-bum (continued)

PLATE 56
The Old Family All-bum (continued)

an auctioneer. He was the town crier and was more or less a howling success, even in his infancy."

(Draw a picture of a safety pin, as in Plate 54.) "This is Miss ————'s *(name of local character)* first beauty pin."

(Draw the bald-pated gentleman of Plate 55.) "And who is this? None other than ———— *(name of local character, a bald-headed man)* when he was a baby. It is quite interesting to note how he has carried that one lone hair down the years. This picture was taken when he was looking for a piece of custard pie in the cake box and found cookies instead. And that, my friends, is why he would never eat crackers in bed."

(Draw the magnifying glass containing the mustache and other features shown in Plate 56.) "A picture of ———— *(local character who has a small or funny-looking mustache)* showing his mustache as seen under the magnifying glass."

"For my concluding picture in the family all-bum, I shall show you a portrait of ———— *(name of a tall man who is popular)* in four chapters." *(Draw the head and upper part of body, as in Plate 57, making as good a likeness in caricature as possible.)* "Chapter one."

(Remove the picture and lay it aside and draw the central part of the body on the next sheet, as in Plate 58.) "Chapter two."

(When this picture is finished remove it, also, and draw the legs on the next sheet of paper, as in Plate 59.) "Chapter three."

(Finally finish by drawing the lower part of the legs and feet, as in Plate 60.) "Chapter four."

PLATE 57
The Old Family All-bum (continued)

PLATE 58
The Old Family All-bum (continued)

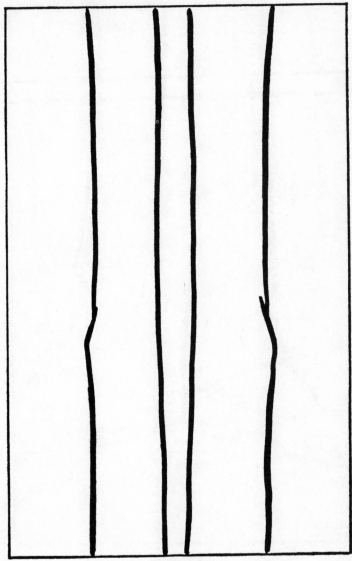

PLATE 59
The Old Family All-bum (continued)

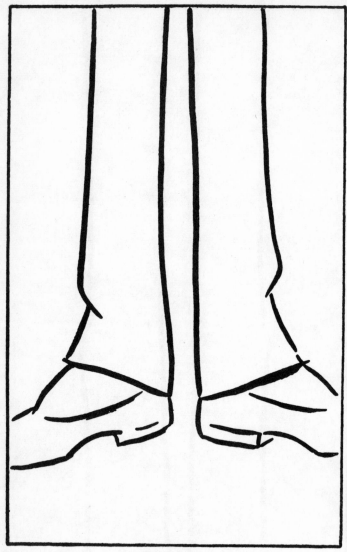

PLATE 60
The Old Family All-bum (concluded)

Another way of handling the pictures in the family album series is to have them already drawn when the chalk talk begins, each on a sheet representing a leaf from the album. As each picture is shown, the artist tells its story, removes it, and goes on to the next. Drawn on heavy cardboard, the pictures will stand on an easel without any difficulty.

Section III
CHALK TALK STUNTS

THE LAZY MAN'S CHALK TALK

(Plate 1)

In order to capture the attention of the audience without delay, it is well for the chalk talker to begin his lecture with some simple novelty whose chief quality is "punch." If it is comic, so much the better.

"The Lazy Man's Chalk Talk" is such a novelty. It calls for a minimum of effort and skill; in fact, it requires no drawing at all! It lends itself to comedy and fits in as an opener for a program, or as a novelty sandwiched in between other pictures.

The artist says:

"I have an artist friend who is so lazy that he hates to get up in the morning because it requires too much effort to go to bed again at night. His attitude towards life has developed a peculiar technique in his drawing. It is the simplest style of drawing that I have ever seen. I will give you examples of how he handles various subjects, the first being:

A BIRD'S-EYE VIEW OF THE SAHARA DESERT."

(*Point to blank paper and, if you desire, bow slightly.*) "There you are: a genuine bird's-eye view of a desert." (*Remove blank sheet of paper.*)

"Now for the second picture I shall draw:
A STREET SCENE SHOWING A CROWD OF SCOTCHMEN ON TAG DAY."
(*Point to blank paper again.*) "There you are

PLATE 1
The Lazy Man's Chalk Talk

again. A perfect picture of Scotchmen on tag day or any other day when a collection is being taken." (*Remove blank sheet of paper.*)

"The next picture is somewhat more difficult and requires considerable care and training in handling. It is called

THE CHILDREN OF ISRAEL FLEEING FROM PHARAOH'S ARMY ACROSS THE RED SEA."

(*Point to blank paper.*) "There is a peculiar rare delicacy in this picture, the color blending being perfect. Pardon me, but did I overhear some one asking as to where the Red Sea is? Washed away. Where are the children of Israel? Gone across. Pharaoh's army? Drowned."

Here are three more subjects for the "Lazy Man's Chalk Talk," which might add variety to your program from time to time:

ILLUSTRATING ELBERT HUBBARD'S BOOK ON "SILENCE"

(*Point to blank paper.*)   "Silence."

A HOLSTEIN COW GRAZING

(*Point to blank paper.*)   "Where is the grass? The cow has eaten it. Where is the cow? Gone to find more grass."

Another variation, after you have three of the subjects on the blank white paper, is to say, "In the next picture let me introduce you to a masterpiece of modern-day art:

NIGHT-TIME IN NORMANDY."

Lift off the blank sheet of white paper and under it have a blank sheet of black paper. It is self-explanatory.

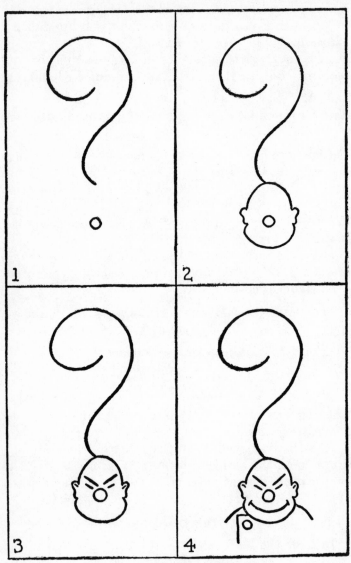

PLATE 2
The Question and the Chinaman

EVOLUTION PICTURES

Evolution pictures are produced by drawing a picture and then with a few strokes of the crayon changing it into something radically different from the original conception. Such a picture never fails to hold the interest of an audience, because it always keeps them on tiptoe with curiosity until the drawing is finished. In the following pages, each illustration has been divided into four figures so that the consecutive steps taken to transform, or evolve, the one picture into the other may be readily seen.

The pictures have been kept as simple as possible, but in spite of their simplicity, they should be drawn repeatedly for practice, prior to the artist's public performance, until he knows every line by heart and is at no loss as to what to do next.

With each illustration are given suggestions for "patter," which may be varied in accordance with the entertainer's program and the locality in which it is given. Local hits, which, if skillfully done, are often popular with audiences, may be introduced into the talk at the entertainer's discretion.

THE QUESTION AND THE CHINAMAN (Plate 2)
(Draw question mark first. Face front.)
> The question is, to bob or not to bob?
>   And what style, if you do.
> You do adore the boyish bob
>   And love the shingled, too.

(Draw while speaking.)
> Rest easy, girls; I'll tell you what
>   A man told me who knew;
> He said, "Next style to grace the fair
>   Will be the Chinese queue."

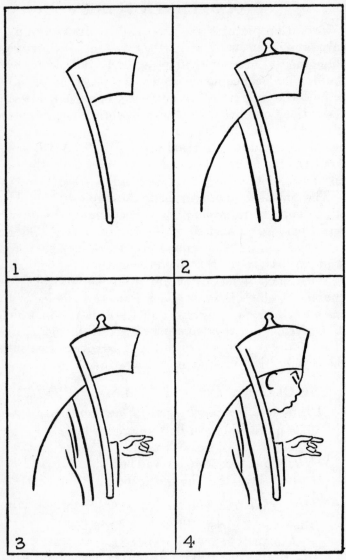

PLATE 3
The Ax and the Executioner

THE AX AND THE EXECUTIONER (Plate 3)

This is the ax of Fu Fu, a Chinese executioner. Fu Fu is about to receive two dollars cash for chopping off the head of one Chu Chu, a Manchurian humorist.

"Good-bye, Chu Chu," said Fu Fu, as he raised the ax. "To-morrow you will have no more head than a pinwheel."

"You are wrong," replied Chu Chu, "for I have just finished drinking a gallon of strong rice wine."

"What does that mean?" inquired the executioner.

"It means," answered Chu Chu, "that no matter what happens to me to-night, I shall have a head on me in the morning."

Fu Fu could not see the point, but Chu Chu, who was very fond of his own jokes, laughed his head off, thus doing Fu Fu out of two dollars.

This is how Fu Fu looks without the two dollars.

HEART AND SWEETHEART (Plate 4)

This is a type of picture that can be done silently. It is self-explanatory. You really write your talk.

Draw a heart. Above it, write H-E-A-R-T. Finish the picture, changing it to a baby. Write S-W-E-E-T in front of HEART.

THE RABBIT AND THE LANTERNS (Plate 5)

Little Johnnie had a bunny, which he fed on milk and
    honey,
But it was a magic animal, and it acted sort of
    funny;
For this tricky little rabbit had an aggravating habit
Of turning into something else when Johnnie tried to
    grab it.

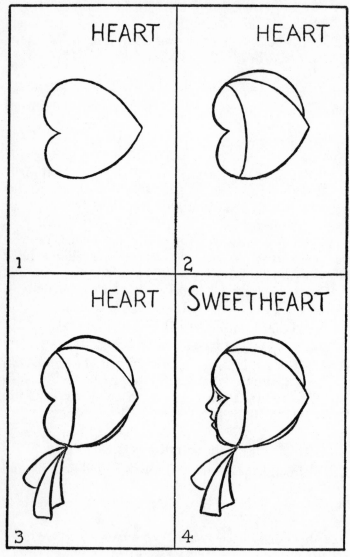

PLATE 4
Heart and Sweetheart

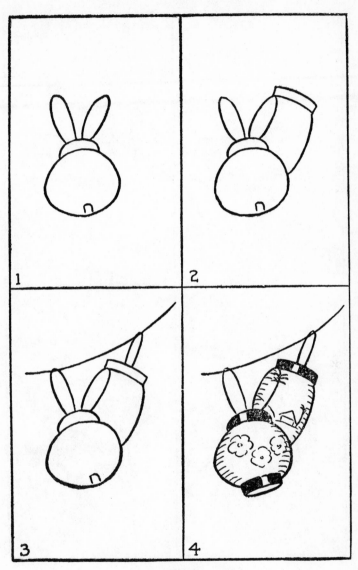

PLATE 5
The Rabbit and the Lanterns

PLATE 6
The Mouse and Towser

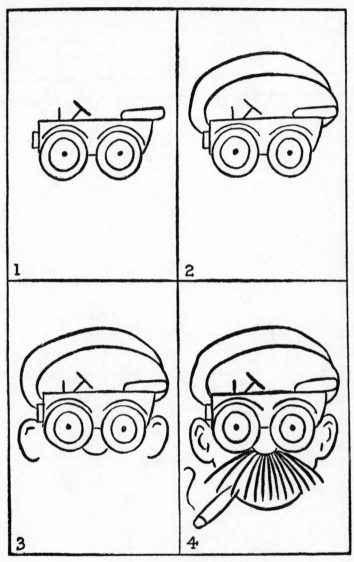

PLATE 7
The Bus and the Driver

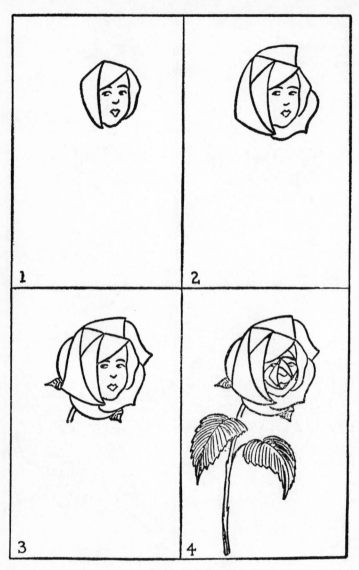

PLATE 8
The Girl and the Rose

He would turn into a parrot; then he'd fly up to the
　　garret,
Where he'd roost upon the rafters while he calmly
　　ate a carrot.
But one night when full of static, just to make it
　　more emphatic,
He turned into Chinese lanterns; now he's hanging
　　in the attic.

THE MOUSE AND TOWSER (Plate 6)

A young mouse in an empty flat
　　Said, "Gosh! I ought to live forever.
No dog or cat or rough-on-rat
　　Can ever get me; I'm too clever!"

A puppy spied this little mouse;
　　(He's what the breeders call a mouser.)
Here's Towser now, inside the house,
　　And here's the mouse, inside of Towser.

THE BUS AND THE DRIVER (Plate 7)

This little car is made of tin,
　　With here and there a rivet.
It runs on gas or tea or gin,
　　Or anything you give it.

It climbs the mountain, fords the brook,
　　Or swims the roaring river.
And this is how you get to look
　　If-you should drive a flivver.

THE GIRL AND THE ROSE (Plate 8)

"Love is blind" is a saying I've heard,
　　But with that I don't quite agree,
For a man in love sees more than he ought;
　　He sees things that others can't see.

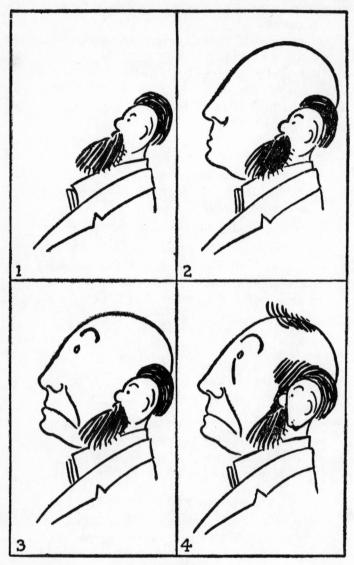

PLATE 9
Lord McGoofus and His Butler

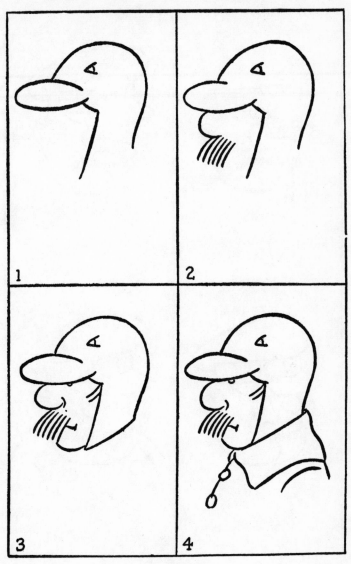

PLATE 10
The Goose and the Farmer

PLATE 11
The Janitor and the Cop

No matter how homely his sweetheart may be
Or how pointed and long her nose,
No matter what faults the others may see,
To him she will look like a rose.

Lord McGoofus and His Butler (Plate 9)

You may omit the patter with this picture. Draw
Lord McGoofus; then with as much speed as possible transform him into the butler. The nature of
the picture enables you to get a surprise finish. Let
your chalk do the work occasionally in a program,
unaccompanied by talk. It gives variety.

The Goose and the Farmer (Plate 10)

Farmer Gray said, one day,
To the goose he meant to slay,
As he grasped the cruel hatchet by the handle,
"Come on, dear, over here,
Let me whisper in your ear;
I can tell you quite a lot of barnyard scandal."

"What's the use?" said the goose,
As she muttered some excuse,
For she knew that apple-knocker meant to harm her.
Then she rose, raining blows
On his eyes and ears and nose.
Now you can't tell which is goose or which is farmer.

What is sauce for the goose is sausage for the farmer.

The Janitor and the Cop (Plate 11)

In this style of evolution picture, you can change
one man into another. It gives you a chance to tell
a joke which employs the two characters. The first
character need not be a janitor. He can represent
a burglar, an engineer, a night watchman, a street-

PLATE 12
The Transformation of Grandpa

car conductor, or any other similar character that you can fit into your joke or story. You can also draw the picture without talk and finish with something on this order: "As Alf, the second-story worker, says, 'It's a wise burglar who doesn't stay where a cop is.' "

THE TRANSFORMATION OF GRANDPA (Plate 12)

My grandpa was a trifle old,
  A little bent and rather thinnish;
But grandpa had a heart of gold
  Which beat beneath his bunch of spinach.

One day he met the Widow Prout,
  And that, alas, was grandpa's finish!
He's getting stout, he's stepping out;
  She took him—heart and gold and spinach!

The foregoing is another type of transformation picture, in which one character changes into another.

THE BABY BUGGY AND DAD (Plate 13)

When daddy wheels this carriage out,
The old-time friends he meets all shout,
"Hey, Bill, old top! I wish you joy!
What's in the buggy? Girl or boy?"

Then dad yells, "Both," and shouts with glee
When each one asks, "How can that be?"
He lifts the carriage robe and grins,
And answers, "How? Because they're twins!"

Observe that this picture has an upside-down feature that explains itself. After it is finished (Fig. 3), it is turned upside down and shown with the head right side up (Fig. 4).

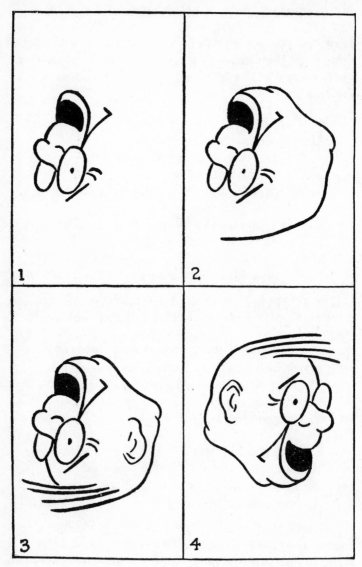

PLATE 13
The Baby Buggy and Dad

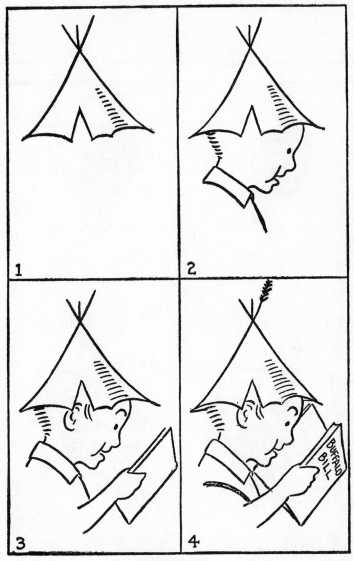

PLATE 14
The Wigwam and the Boy

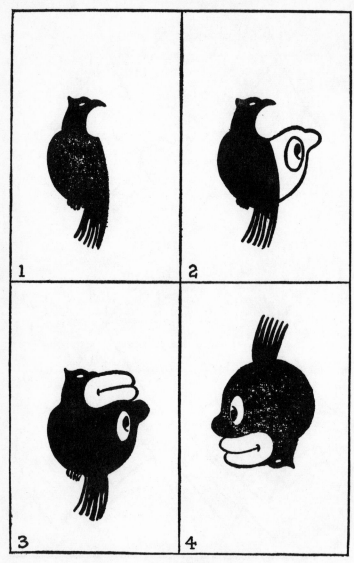

PLATE 15
The Snoffeljee and the Hottentot

THE WIGWAM AND THE BOY (Plate 14)

Behold! The wigwam of the brave!
    The warrior's tent, the chief's tepee!
Behold a boy whose name is Dave,
    The same as Crocket's used to be.

He seeks adventures, poor boy scout!
    And yearns for some to come his way;
But, shucks! What thrills can chaps get out
    Of doing one good deed each day?

Upon a book he's often read
    His eager, childish gaze is bent.
The tent is now on Davy's head,
    And that is why he is intent.

THE SNOFFELJEE AND THE HOTTENTOT (Plate 15)

A wonderful bird is the Snoffeljee;
    It builds its nest in the waffle tree,
        And all day long
        It warbles this song:
"I'm free! Oh, gee! I'm glad I'm free!"

This wonderful bird cannot be caught;
    You can't tell whether he's shot or not.
        When you think he's dead
        He will stand on his head
    (*Turn picture upside down.*)
And turn right into a Hottentot.

(*Hold picture up for audience to see.*)

This is another evolution picture with an upside-down feature. After the picture is finished (Fig. 3),

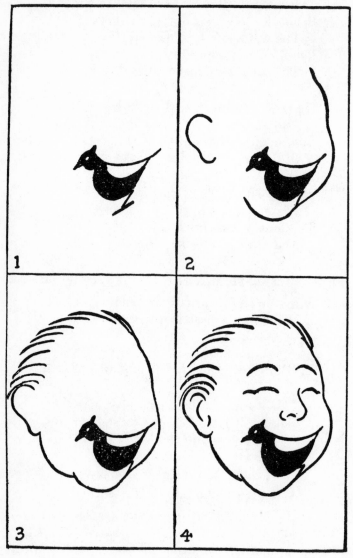

PLATE 16
The Bird and the Man

PLATE 17
The Squaw and the Squawker

PLATE 18
The Witch and the Dove

turn it over (Fig. 4), and hold it up long enough for the audience to get a good view of it.

THE BIRD AND THE MAN (Plate 16)

At times the kind of language used in a primary school book gives a certain "punch" to a chalk picture.

(*Draw bird.*)

Is this a bird?

Yes, this is a bird.

It is a black bird with white wings.

Is the bird sitting on a twig? (*Fig. 2.*)

Yes, he is sitting on the limb of a tree.

Look! The limb of the tree has leaves on it. (*Fig. 3.*)

And this is the man who laughed at the bird who sat on the limb of the tree with leaves on it. Ha, ha! Ho, ho! (*Fig. 4.*)

THE SQUAW AND THE SQUAWKER (Plate 17)

Similar to the "Heart and Sweetheart" picture, this one also requires no patter. Chalk the talk. Draw the Indian and write above her, S-Q-U-A-W. Finish as in Figure 4 and add K-E-R to the word SQUAW.

THE WITCH AND THE DOVE (Plate 18)

(*Draw witch. Face front.*)

Now you think, of course, I've drawn a witch,
  And surely seeing is believing.
But you just watch me finish this
  And see how chalk talks are deceiving.

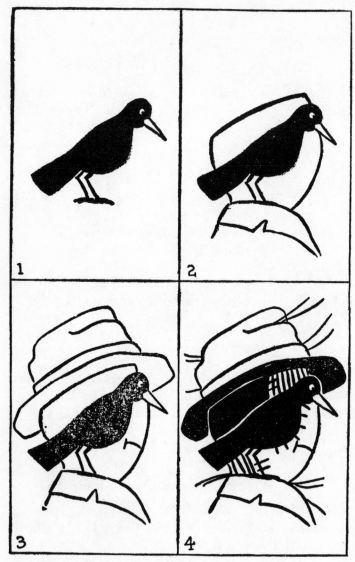

PLATE 19
The Crow and the Scarecrow

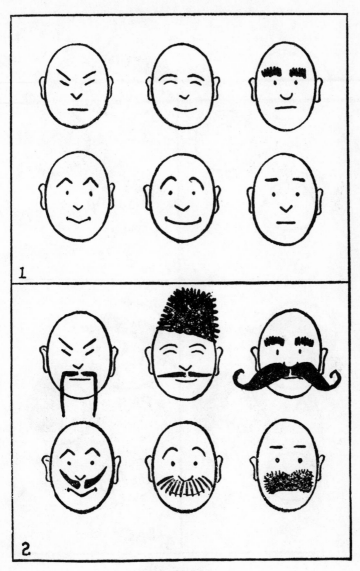

PLATE 20
By Their Mustaches Ye Shall Know Them

PLATE 21
The Evolution of a Family

(Draw.)

    Hocus-pocus! I'll add this line
      And then another just above.
    Here goes a curve, and there you are!
      My magic makes the witch a dove.

The Crow and the Scarecrow (Plate 19)

    I've tried and tried to keep this crow
      Away from my garden patch.
    She eats my lettuce and my kale;
      Her wits I cannot match.

    But at last I've found a man who can,
      Who'll guard it night and day.
    Though his brain is naught but straw and hay,
      He'll keep that crow away.

By Their Mustaches Ye Shall Know Them (Plate 20)

Every type of character is distinguished by certain physical traits, by which it may be recognized at a glance. This fact is the basis of this stunt. First, draw the six heads. As the paper is longer than it is wide, it may be necessary to vary the arrangement by placing two heads in a horizontal line and three up and down. Then say to the audience, "By their mustaches ye shall know them," and add the mustache and other trimmings to each head in turn. This stunt never fails to delight an audience.

The Evolution of a Family (Plate 21)

Figure 1 represents a grapefruit, and orange, and a lemon. They will be twice as effective if they are appropriately colored. Flat tones of color should

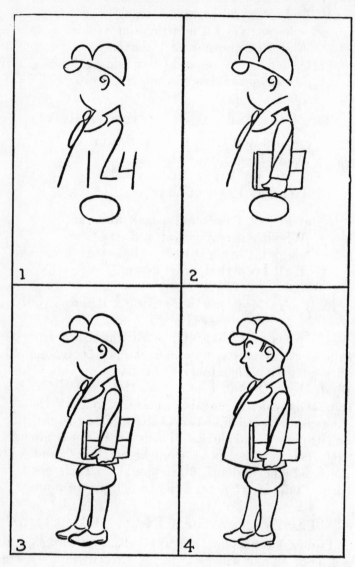

PLATE 22
A Stunt with Numbers

be used, and applied with the flat side of the chalk. Yellow will give the proper tone to the grapefruit and the lemon, and orange to the orange. Figures 2, 3, and 4 show the various steps in drawing necessary to complete the family group.

This family stunt was first utilized in a talk given before the salesmen of an orange drink manufacturing concern. On that occasion, an orange, a lemon, and a lime were used to represent the three drinks they were featuring; namely, orangeade, lemonade, and limeade. The problem before the company at that time was to get its salesmen to push the two latter drinks, as well as the first. Orangeade had been put on the market first. It sold well, so the average salesman was satisfied to feature it alone without the other two. Limeade was the newest— the baby of the three. Thus the family idea was evolved and worked out in the following manner: Pictures of an orange, a lemon, and a lime were drawn, and the orange was transformed into pa, the lemon into ma, and the lime into the baby, thus completing the Ade family.

The lecturer said to the salesmen, "Whenever any of you go into a store and see only orangeade on sale, ask the dealer where ma and the baby are. When he asks who ma and the baby are, tell him the story of the Ade family. Say that they live the most happily when they are together, that pa fares best when ma is around, and that ma gets lonesome without the baby. As for the baby, even though limeade is a baby now, it is bound to grow and may some day even outgrow pa and ma."

This story is told to show how important a part chalk talks may be made to play in business. The same comedy stunt that serves to amuse an audience

PLATE 23
A Six Percenter

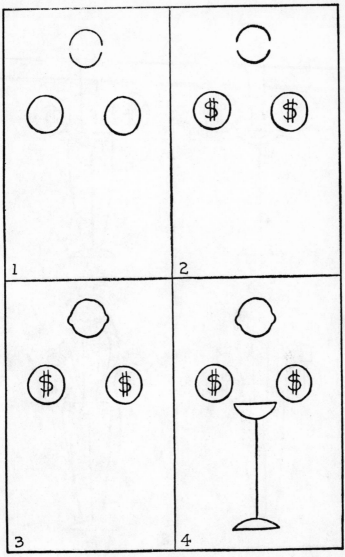

PLATE 24
The Evolution of a Duke

PLATE 25
The Evolution of a Duke (concluded)

in its idle moments may also be applied to the solution of serious problems in business. Novelty stunts are easy to remember. A limerick sticks longer in the popular memory than a classical quotation; for the average human being does not mind absorbing knowledge, if it only be simple and entertaining.

A Stunt with Numbers (Plate 22)

All the numbers from 1 to 9, including 0, are used in this stunt. Figure 1 shows the arrangement, while Figure 4 exhibits the finished product.

A Six Percenter (Plate 23)

Here again is a self-explanatory comedy picture. After the 6% has been drawn, speed up the rest of the picture until Figure 4 is produced.

The Evolution of a Duke (Plates 24, 25)

This picture will always be popular with audiences because of the number of transformations and the simplicity by which they are brought about. Its appeal is dependent on the power of suggestion.

The artist says to the audience:

"Many times while I am drawing, I hear a person in the audience wonder about what I am making as I go along and what the finished picture will be. I shall endeavor to show you the thoughts that pass through such a mind as I draw this next picture."

(*Draw the upper circle. Fig. 1.*) "Oh, isn't that a nice moon?"

(*Draw two more circles. Fig. 1.*) "But why make three moons?"

(*Put dollar signs on lower circles. Fig. 2.*)

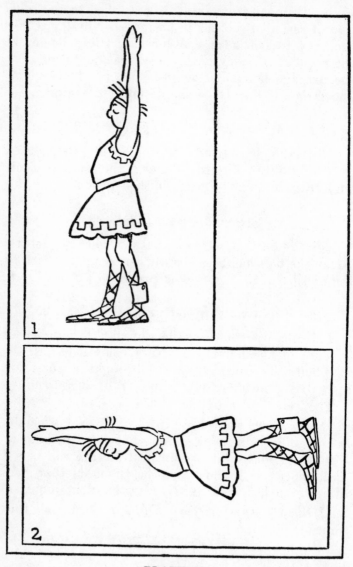

PLATE 26
Roman Art

"Why, of course, now that he has put dollar signs on the moons, they aren't moons. They are a pawnbroker's sign—three balls."

(*Change the upper circle into a lemon. Fig. 3.*) "But what has a lemon got to do with a pawnbroker's sign?"

(*Draw a glass. Fig. 4.*) "Yes, yes. Now that he has made a glass, the lemon is to make lemonade, and there is the money to pay for it. Or maybe it's a juggling performance, where the juggler throws things into the air."

(*Draw two lemonade straws. Fig. 5.*) "Guess that's right, because he's balanced the lemon on two lemonade straws. Or maybe those are the lemonade straws to drink the lemonade with."

(*Draw a large glass. Fig. 6.*) "That's a good idea. Give us a good big glass for lemonade—one of the circus kind."

(*Draw hands and a hat. Fig. 7.*) "That looks like a bug or an insect of some kind. See the funny-looking head and the eyes it has. It might be a wire puzzle or a futurist picture."

(*Quick finish. Fig. 8.*) "There! I knew what it was, all the time. It's a foreign duke with some American girl's money, unless it is a bootlegger or a magician."

ROMAN ART
(Plates 26, 27)

Because of the peculiar nature of this picture, it will fit almost any place in a program where a novelty is needed. It is a single picture that adapts itself to many uses.

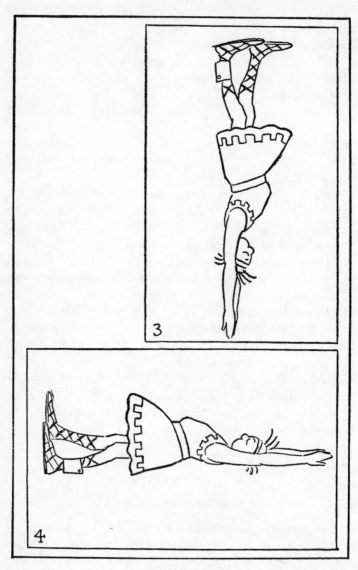

PLATE 27
Roman Art (concluded)

PLATE 28
The God of the Sea and the Ship

PLATE 29
A Thanksgiving Suggestion

PLATE 30
A Christmas Suggestion

PLATE 31
A New Year's Suggestion

The artist says:

"Julius Caesar used to run a newspaper in Rome. On his staff was a cartoonist—a good cartoonist, but lazy. He would rather take in moving picture shows or bullfights than worry over a cartoon. Invention is born of necessity, 'tis said, so this was his idea of a pleasant means of newspaper illustrating."

(*Draw a Roman. Fig. 1.*) "A Roman orator has delivered a speech, so this is the portrait the cartoonist made of him." (*Turn picture on its side. Fig. 2.*) "Next day there was a famous swimming match, so the cartoonist turned the picture this way and headed it 'Brutus Swimming'." (*Turn the picture to upside-down position. Fig. 3.*) "The next day acrobats were at the Coliseum. Picture of an acrobat." (*Turn the picture on its side. Fig. 4.*) "And last but not least, a Roman funeral. Here is the Roman dead."

UPSIDE DOWN STUNT

THE GOD OF THE SEA AND THE SHIP (Plate 28)

Draw the god of the sea (Fig. 1). After you have finished, step aside for a few moments to give audience a good view. Then take the paper off the board and turn it upside down, and the ship (Fig. 2) comes into view.

HOLIDAY SUGGESTIONS
(Plates 29, 30, 31)

Three suggestions are given for Thanksgiving, Christmas, and New Year's Day respectively. The drawing is shown, step by step, so you should have

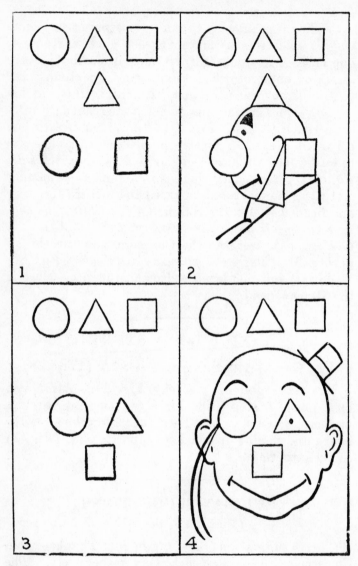

PLATE 32
The Circle, the Triangle, and the Square

PLATE 33
The Circle, the Triangle, and the Square (continued)

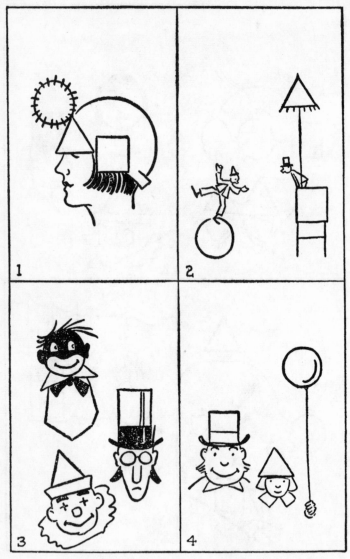

PLATE 34
The Circle, the Triangle, and the Square (continued)

no difficulty in making the pictures. Some color here
and there would help them. These pictures show up
especially well on a heavy gray paper, when drawn
with black, white, and colored chalks.   ..

THE CIRCLE, THE TRIANGLE, AND THE SQUARE
(Plates 32 to 36)

This is an excellent stunt to show audience your
power of imagination, your speed of mentality, and
your ability to meet an emergency. To an audience
it seems very difficult as you do not know what will
happen in advance and your success depends on
your clever way of handling things. In reality, the
circle, triangle, and square stunt is easy. Once you
know the laws governing it, you need never be caught
napping or fear the outcome. For this reason, it
permits good showmanship.

You ask for any gentleman in the audience to
come to the stage to assist you. When he is on the
platform and you have shaken hands with him, you
take him over to your board and say, "Now, sir, I
am going to draw a circle, a triangle, and a square."
You draw them at the top of the paper (Plate 32).
You continue: "I want you also to draw a similar
circle, triangle, and square; but arrange them any
way you desire. Put a circle in one place, a triangle
in another, and a square in another, any way, any
place, near together, far apart, up above, down below, on the sides of the paper, any way to suit your
fancy, just as long as you make them on the paper."

After the assistant has made the figures, you continue talking: "To me everything suggests a picture. There are hundreds, and maybe thousands,

PLATE 35
The Circle, the Triangle, and the Square (continued)

of ways that the gentleman could arrange a circle, a triangle, and a square. This particular style of arrangement, however, suggests this picture to me."

You take the crayon and with a few lines change the figures into a picture of some kind. Plates 32, 33, 34, 35, and 36 show what can be done with various combinations.

You can repeat the stunt two or three times. It is not necessary for you to draw a circle, triangle, and square on each paper. You did this on the first one merely to instruct the assistant as to what to do and at the same time to help keep the figures somewhat in proportion. Ordinarily, it is best to let the assistant draw them any size or in any proportion to one another that he wants. It gives the artist a better chance to use his imagination.

The secret is easy. It requires just a little common sense. Study the various arrangements in Plates 32, 33, 34, 35, and 36 and see how they are handled. There are two methods of handling. One is to use the figures combined to form one picture (Plate 32), while the other is to turn each figure into a separate object. For examples of this, see Plate 33, Figures 2 and 4; also Plate 34, Figures 3 and 4. The better way, of course, is to draw the circle, triangle, and square combined into one figure; but the other method saves the day when the mind does not work quickly enough to use the first method with skill and ingenuity.

Your audience never knows what you are going to do in advance. In this respect, you are like a magician. Therefore you can master the situation for yourself, and what the audience doesn't know about what you might have done will not hurt it any.

PLATE 36
The Circle, the Triangle, and the Square (concluded)

The triangle-circle-and-square stunt is a pleasing variation from the dot pictures described in "How to Chalk Talk," in which the performer makes pictures from any combination of dots placed on the paper by one of the audience.

In your moments of leisure, take a pencil and paper and let anyone draw a circle, a triangle, and a square. Then see what you can do with the combination. New ideas perhaps will suggest themselves. Practice gives confidence.

EASY HUMAN FIGURE DRAWING FOR CHALK TALKS

The human figure is by no means an easy thing to draw when made in photographic proportions. Therefore let me suggest a method that gives "punchy" figure drawing with more ease of accomplishment. Observe closely Plates 37 to 41. Note the large-head-and-small-body idea and the simplicity in drawing the head. Many times, a mere circle with the features added answers the purpose and may create a greater impression than if you made a photographic reproduction. This simple style of drawing shows much action with but a few lines. This style of cartooning or caricature enables you to accent features and points you want to bring out and to avoid characteristics you do not want. Just a few lines, and you have told your story.

AN EASY WAY TO DRAW AN AFTER-DINNER SPEAKER (Plate 37)

Start with an ellipse or circle. Fig. 1 shows how to draw it by drawing curve on left side and then drawing balance on right hand side. Then fill in

PLATE 37
An Easy Way to Draw an After-Dinner Speaker

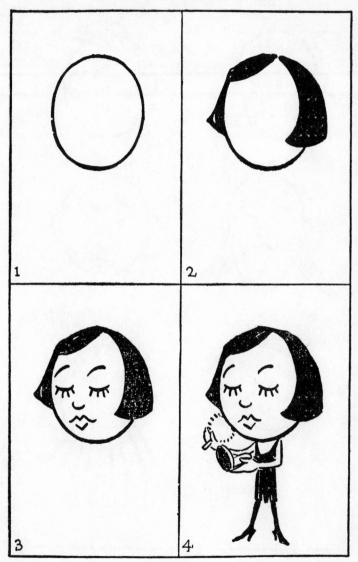

PLATE 38
An Easy Way to Draw a Flapper

PLATE 39
A Few Expressions

PLATE 40
An Easy Way to Draw Men

PLATE 41
An Easy Way to Draw Women

eyes, nose, eyebrows, mouth, ears, hair, and finally body, table, and objects thereon. Behold! An after-dinner speaker or toastmaster of some kind.

An Easy Way to Draw a Flapper (Plate 38)

This is the flapper. Easy to draw, step by step.

A Few Expressions (Plate 39)

For drawing facial expressions, just a few lines, and there you are. Study the magazines of humor, also the comic sections of newspapers, and see how various characteristics are expressed. Notice cartoons, and see how the cartoonist gets his expression and action. Then follow his methods and simplify them for chalk talks.

An Easy Way to Draw Men and Women (Plates 40, 41)

Here we have figures of men and women in action, showing the effective use of large expressive heads and small bodies.

CHALK TALK PHASES OF THE WORLD WAR

Out of the tragedy of the world war has come considerable comedy. The comic side of the war is very popular and will grow more so as the years pass. An artist may chalk-talk the funny things of the war and make a very interesting program. A talk of this nature would be well suited to some American Legion entertainment. It may also be successfully featured before practically any audience. If the artist has been overseas, so much the better, as he can add a personal touch to his work and talk from experience. It is not the purpose of this book

PLATE 42
The Mountain and the Doughboy

to offer a prepared lecture. It is better to give sugtions, by means of which the entertainer may build
his own talk.

A little study of the subject will doubtless help
him to find many interesting features of the war that
he can easily turn into pictures. If he has been
through the war himself, he probably has hundreds
of experiences that can readily be recalled.

But whether he has been to war or not, he may
chalk talk the comedy of the war, for which he will
find a receptive audience.

THE MOUNTAIN AND THE DOUGHBOY (Plate 42)

This is an evolution picture showing how a young
mountain with a cloud passing by can be changed to
comic action. The idea was suggested to the author
upon his seeing Mount Sec (where a great battle was
fought) as he was strolling along from Heudicourt
on the way to Nonsard Woods.

For patter, use something like this: "Is this a
beautiful mountain with a cloud rolling gently by?"
(*Finish drawing. Fig. 2.*) "No. It is a doughboy
hugging the earth while a shell bursts and a G. I.
can goes by." (A G. I. can is a nickname given to
a type of shell about the size of a garbage can.)

DOUGHBOY STUDIES (Plate 43)

Fig. 1.—This sketch, drawn from life, is of an old-
timer who had been an army man for nineteen years,
had been through the Philippine war, and had once
been a captain. His delight was "second looies"
(second lieutenants), and it was very amusing at
times to see them try to order him around. He always spoke affectionately of the "second looies" as
"ninety-day wonders" (three months being required

PLATE 43
Doughboy Studies

for training). Wiler was a sergeant, but he felt
more at home as a buck private and was more content to be acting cook and to smoke a pipe than to
order the boys around.

Fig. 2.—Shorty Bobbins had more troubles than
a dog has fleas. "Aw, quit yer growling," the boys
would say to him; to which he would reply, "I ain't
growling; I'm just tellin' yez." One day the company was taken over to Commercy for shower baths.
That evening Shorty was in very good humor because when he had taken his bath that day, he had
found in the leg of his underwear his "dog tags"
(identification tags which were hung by string
around the neck) which he had lost track of for
about two months. It was reported around among
the boys that Shorty could walk under a bureau
when he was a baby, and even yet he was so short
that it was hard for him to reach up high enough to
comb his own hair. At least his hair was seldom
combed, and that was as good a reason as any.

Fig. 3.—Here is "the latest news." Of all the
rumors, tips, and private information that the world
has ever had, it has had nothing on those that came
out of the war. A soldier was as hungry for news
as the farmer who used to come to town twice a day
after the weekly paper. An inch of news could
stretch to full-sized edition of a newspaper in about
an hour. Every time it was retold, it grew just that
much larger. When report said the troops were going to move fast, they didn't move at all, and when
the news spread that they were settled there for the
winter, the signal came to move within the hour.
After the armistice was signed, word came that the
whole company would be home by Christmas, but
needless to say, it was the following September when

PLATE 44
More Doughboy Studies

the boys next gazed upon the **Statue of Liberty.**
That accounts for

Figure 4 and the national anthem, "We Wanta
Go Home," which arose as a result of the delay in
travel. The gang was "leaving next week" from
November until the following September—a positive
fact, as the news "came straight from headquar-
ters"; at least that is what everyone but head-
quarters said. Captain White used to say, "A soldier is a funny creature. He is hungry to get to a
place, and when he gets there he wants to be somewhere else."

More Doughboy Studies (Plate 44)

Fig. 1.—There was sick call every morning, when,
as Sergeant Wiler used to say, "the halt, the lame,
and the blind used to come around to see if there
wasn't a possible chance of escaping work for the
day." Naturally anyone would feel sorry for this
young soldier in the picture, who was rushing to sick
call as fast as his legs could carry him because, as
he explained to the doctor, "My rheumatism is so
bad that I can hardly walk. Somebody may have to
carry me back to the bunk so I can lie in bed all day."

Fig. 2.—Here is a typical scene in many a barrack
with a leaky roof—a case of room and bath together.
Now and then, some budding poet would give vent
to his feelings thusly:

> "Mother, may I go out to swim?
>   Yes, my darling son.
> Go to bed on a rainy night;
>   Gosh, ain't we got fun?"

"I say, old man, have you taken your bawth?"
"Yeh; taken it right to bed with me."

PLATE 45
Joys and Sorrows of the Doughboy

PLATE 46
The Ideal and the Real

PLATE 47
Doughboy Dreams

Joys and Sorrows of the Doughboy (Plate 45)

Fig. 1.—Many a letter received in camp showed anxiety on the part of some girl back home who was worrying because some beautiful French mademoiselle would steal her loved one's heart away. Here is a sketch from life of two of the most beautiful girls in the vicinity of the American army. No; the boys were not in Paris at the time.

Fig. 2.—Have you ever heard of the "American twins" and the "French twins"? It surely didn't take them very long to get acquainted. As Sergeant O'Gillilan said, "A good time was had by all."

The Ideal and the Real (Plate 46)

This picture speaks for itself. It might be called "In the Land of Might Have Been" or "If I Was What I Ain't Instead of What I Is."

"You're in the army now,
   You're not behind a plow,
   What might have been, you surely ain't;
   You're in the army now."

Doughboy Dreams (Plate 47)

Fig. 1.—Did you ever sleep in a French bed? The kind you have to take a high dive to get into? And then bury yourself between two feather ticks about seventeen times thicker than any you had ever seen at home? And then you sank down so far into the bottom tick that it took you ten minutes to find yourself the next morning. Quite a bit different from the old pup tent or the barracks bed. The "ayes" have it. All votes to the contrary not counted.

In drawing this picture, color the bed ticks red,

IN TIME FOR
CHOW

PLATE 48
French Peasant Types

Fig. 2.—There are some languages that no one seems to understand, and then again there are languages of which everyone seems to have a good understanding, regardless of creed, nationality, or education. This is one of the latter. As the poet says,

> "Voo aimee mwa;*
> I love you.
> No knife can cut
> Our love in two."

French Peasant Types (Plate 48)

The figures on this plate, as well as the next one, were sketched from life in a little French village not far from Commercy, where some American troops were stationed for about a month. The peasants' real names were never known to the boys, who christened the former to suit themselves.

Fig. 1.—"Delicacy." This is "Boy Blue's" wife. She used to wear a bright blue dress and every morning go by with sheep to take out for a day's grazing. "Little Boy Blue" was a man with long white whiskers, somewhere between the ages of five years and four hundred and sixty-seven years. He wore a blue cap, a blue overcoat with brass buttons, and a big vari-colored muffler around his neck, and carried a tin horn. He used to drive and herd the sheep.

Fig. 2.—"Old Man Enthusiasm." An exponent of acrobatic dancing. He could go a mile in three days if he hurried.

Fig. 3.—"Nameless." We couldn't find a name for this one. Much to our surprise, he had never

---

*Doughboy French.

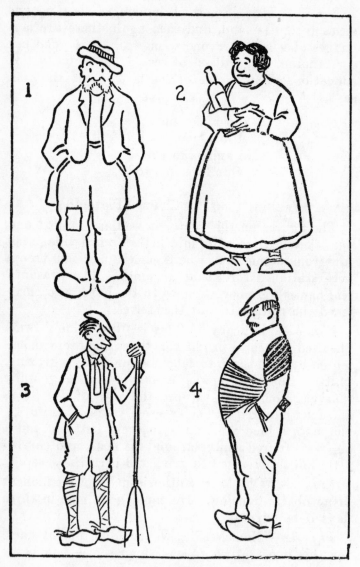

PLATE 49
More French Peasant Types

heard of Egypt, Illinois, or the stockyards of Chicago.

Fig. 4.—"Snick-en-poodle." A little youngster who came around at mealtime with a pan to be filled with "chow." She became a great friend of Eddie the cook, who was always on the lookout at mealtime for his regular customer.

More French Peasant Types (Plate 49)

Fig. 1.—"Peaceful Feathers." He would have been a banker, if the town had a bank and his inclinations had run that way and he had had enough money to start one with. He never objected to the boys' "settin' 'em up" or treating him to cigarettes or tobacco of any kind.

Fig. 2.—"Mrs. Vin Blink." Hostess to the boys with "vin blanc" and "vin rouge." She never refused money. She was a favorite of the "soldats" on pay day.

Fig. 3.—"Classics." A hero, a poet, or a general—the boys could not decide which. He'd have been a "go-getter," if there had been anything to get.

Fig. 4.—"Mr. Vin Blink." Mrs. Vin Blink's husband. He could stand in one spot longer than anyone else in town. He took great pride in seeing Mrs. Vin Blink collect money from the "soldats américains."

Sight-Seeing in Paris (Plate 50)

What would the war have been without Paris—Paris, with its mademoiselles, gendarmes, M.P.'s (military police), and cabbies? Yes, Paris with its Y.M.C.A. wagon, Red Cross canteen, Montmartre, A.W.O.L.'s, Café de la Paix, English-American Offi-

PLATE 50
Sight-seeing in Paris

cers' Club (few could find it—it moved so often), Napoleon's tomb, the museum of wax figures, and the streets that change names every two blocks. There is only one Paris; but, oh, what a Paris!

NOTE.—In chalk talking plates relative to the war, it is well to use a separate sheet of paper for each figure. Avoid crowding your drawing. In some places, colors help out considerably. It is remarkable, sometimes, how a bit of color here and there adds interest to a program and makes the picture stand out.

A NOVELTY TELEPHONE STUNT
(Plate 51)

The artist walks up to the board and draws a picture of a telephone. A bell is heard to ring. The artist takes the receiver off the hook and holds a conversation. This is one of those unexpected effects that an audience likes. It is very easy to do. It requires a little preparation.

Study Plate 51 closely. Get a piece of cardboard and paint on it, with black ink or paint, the picture of a receiver. Cut this picture out with the scissors, and paint the other side of it black also. Take a piece of black tape or cord about two feet long and glue or sew one end to the receiver, and on the other end sew a thumb tack securely. Press a second thumb tack into the end of the receiver.

Have the cardboard receiver and the piece of tape in your vest pocket or some other convenient place where it is easy to get at, but where it is concealed from the audience.

Walk up to the board and draw a telephone box

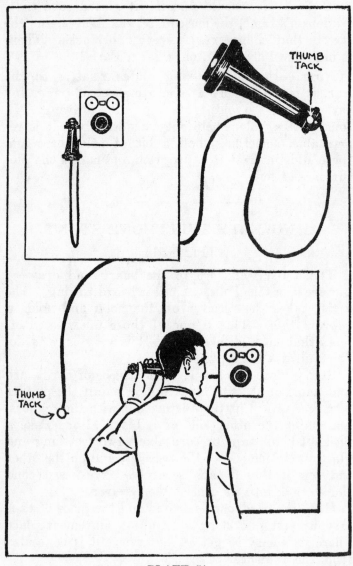

PLATE 51
A Novelty Telephone Stunt

and a receiver hook; then under cover of your body, fasten the receiver and the end of the tape to the board with the thumb tacks. To the audience, the effect looks as if you had drawn the receiver and tape. They didn't see you draw these objects, as your body was in the way; but you have a piece of chalk in your hand and you have been drawing, so there is no apparent reason why you didn't draw the receiver and tape. Being black, they look o. k.

On the back of board have a bicycle bell or electric bell fastened. When ready for the phone to ring, push the button. The bell rings, and you then take off the receiver from the board, hold it to your ear, and hold a one-sided comedy conversation, something on this order:

"Hello. Yes, this is the wrong number. . . Oh, is that you, August? . . How's August? . . That's good, August. . . Is that so, August? . . Yes, August. . . I guess so, August. . . Go ahead, August. . . Of course, August. . . Count, on me, August. . . Fine, August. . . See you later, August. . . Glad you called up, August. Good-bye, August."

Then turn to audience as you hang up the receiver and say, "That was August talking." Just as if they didn't know! This goes well with the name of a local character.

A variation on this conversation is, instead of saying good-bye, to have August leave the phone a moment, and you tell the audience who is talking. When he returns, continue conversation something like this:

"Back again, August? . . Is that so? No, I hadn't heard it. . . Who? Mrs. Hooligan? (*Or name some local character.*) . . . Two of them? . .

When did it happen? . .   Seven o'clock this morning! . .   Did they take her to the hospital? . . I wonder what Hooligan will say? . .   How is Mrs. Hooligan getting along? . .   That's fine, August. Two is better than three. . .   Yes. Uh-huh. Goodbye, August."

Turn to the audience.   By this time, they have been led by their imaginations and the tone of the conversation to conclude that Mrs. Hooligan has had twins; but tell them: "August said that Mrs. Hooligan's pet poodle bit two of her fingers at 7:30 this morning, but it isn't serious, and she will be all right in a few days."

A telephone conversation permits of many brain twists, and it is a comic twist that makes an audience laugh.

COLORING A PICTURE
(Plates 52 to 55)

In making a colored picture, use a heavy paper that has a rough enough surface to take the crayon well.   There is a regular chalk-talk paper for colored pictures, which is gray in color and well suited to chalk work.   For ordinary purposes, ordinary newspaper stock will answer the purpose, but for high grade color pictures you should use a good grade of stock.   Some chalk talkers occasionally use regular book cover stock, which may be picked up at the printer's in various colors.   Many art stores handle regular chalk-talk paper or can advise you where to get it.

The various stages of coloring a picture are as follows:

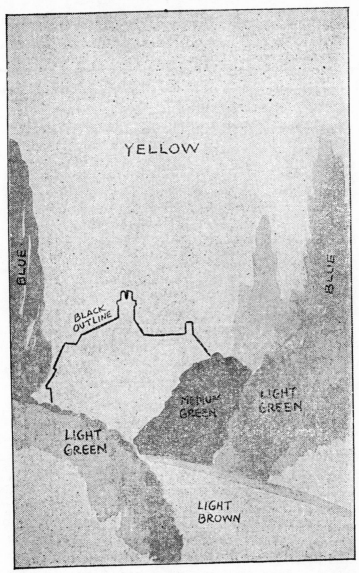

PLATE 52
Coloring a Picture (first stage)

PLATE 53
Coloring a Picture (second stage)

PLATE 54
Coloring a Picture (third stage)

PLATE 55
Coloring a Picture (fourth stage)

Plate 52.—With yellow chalk, put the sky on first, covering the surface well and smoothing down with a wad of cotton. Blend in a bit of blue at the top of the picture to represent blue sky. Draw light green foliage to the left of the picture, then light green on the right, following with medium green. Draw a road of light brown, then blue for the tree at the left and blue for trees at right. With black chalk, outline the house.

Plate 53.—Put in black trees back of the house, then purple and dark green trees. With dark green chalk come down to the foreground and draw foliage on the left and the right sides.

Plate 54.—Fill in the house, making a red roof and colored windows. A little orange in window lights indicates a light inside the house.

Plate 55.—You are now ready for the figures. Draw a man first, and then a woman. Use dark brown for his clothes. Use yellow for her hat, with a touch of green or black, black shawl, and light blue dress with a little brown and green tone for ruffles. His hair should be black, and her hair light in color.

Incidental music adds an effective touch, when you are making a colored picture.

There are a great variety of delightful pictures you can make with colors. You can find many which you can utilize from magazines, post cards, and prints. You can also take an endless number of scenes from nature itself.

In covering large areas with color, it is well to draw with the side of the chalk.

A Youthful Chalk Talker

One of the encouraging things about learning the art of chalk talking is the ease with which children have been known to master it. With no more equipment than a fair degree of talent for drawing, and plenty of industry and enthusiasm, they have achieved amazing success.

Consider the example of Ella Marie White, who became interested in chalk talking at the age of nine and, securing a copy of "How to Chalk Talk," prepared herself for platform work in a surprisingly short time. To-day she is an accomplished amateur chalk talker, quite at home in public performances, in which she displays that professional technique so difficult to teach the amateur. Her work has an original touch not found in that of many chalk talkers, for she writes her own "patter," chiefly in verse, in the composition of which she shows quite as much facility as in the use of her crayons.

Specimens of her rhymed "patter" will be found in connection with several of the illustrations in this book, namely, "The Question and the Chinaman," "The Girl and the Rose," "The Witch and the Dove," and "The Crow and the Scarecrow." (See pages 20, 28, 42, and 44.)